The Man Behind the Mask

D.T.

The Man Behind the Mask

Copyright © 2016 D.T. All rights reserved.

Cover Photo copyright © 2016 D.T. All rights reserved.

ISBN: 0692739076

ISBN-13: 978-0692739075

Unless otherwise indicated, all scripture quotations are taken from the King James Version.

Scripture quotations marked (NIV) are taken from the HOLY BIBLE, NEW INTERNATIONAL VERSION. Copyright © 1973, 1978, 1984 by International Bible Society. Used by permission of Zondervan. All rights reserved.

Dedicated to:

God
You are my loving Father, the source of my life.
My close companion, the love of my life.
My faithful guide, full of true wisdom.
I cannot imagine living without feeling your nearness or hearing the sound of your voice. You have captured my heart. Thank you for being a friend and never letting go.

&

All of you who have played a part in my life.
I was going to list every one of you who have significantly impacted my life, but the list was endless. Whether you are included within the pages of this book or not, please know that I am grateful. You never know how even a "little thing" can change the course of a person's life. Thank you for your friendship, encouragement, and faithfulness along life's journey.

Contents

Introduction 1

Part 1: The Early Years

1. Innocence Lost 5

Part 2: Teen Years

2. The Tug of War 17
3. Spiritual Growth 29

Part 3: College Days

4. The Shock 37
5. Still in God's Hands 45

Part 4: Young Adult Years

6. Living 57
7. Dying 67
8. Learning of Him 89

Part 5: Yielding to God

9. Being Led by God 113
10. Doing Life with God 129
11. No Turning Back 143
12. Returning to Love 153

The Story Continues 169

Into the Light

With each passing day, our life stories unfold
But what good is a story, if it goes untold?
From behind our fears, and hidden tears
Are endless stories, that fill our years.

Through times of boredom, bliss, and terror
And lingering regret, from our times of error.
Our lives are stories, that should be shared,
But for this to happen, our lives we must bare.

We all have struggles, and we all have sinned,
But what matters now, is for new life to begin.
We can wallow in shame, or hide in our pride,
But at the end of the day, we all must decide.

Will we live our lives, in the darkness to hide,
Or will we come to the light, and the cleansing tide?
For freedom is found, in knowing the One
The One from above, who sent us his Son.

He is the One, who came to the earth
And humbled himself, both in death and in birth.
To show us his love, and rewrite our stories
And now he invites us, to share in his glories.

D.T.

Introduction

The Man Behind the Mask is my story. Actually, it is his story. And when I say "his," I mean God's. You see, for many years I questioned the very existence of God. And even after I experienced God, I had some dark times in my life that made me wonder if he had forsaken me. While I did not realize it at the time, I now see God was walking with me the entire way.

My parents were very religious. They taught me a lot of things about God during my early years, but it was not until my teen years that I began to develop a relationship with him. And, it was not until I was a young adult that I really began to follow him.

I would consider myself to have been a "whitewashed tomb" during my early teen years. What I mean by this is what Jesus talked about in Matthew 23:27. He angered the religious leaders by calling them whitewashed tombs. He accused them of being beautiful on the outside while being filled with dead men's bones, hypocrisy, and sin.

I know what it is to be a whitewashed tomb. I know what it is to go through the religious motions while being full of sin on the inside. Growing up, everyone around me thought I was the "perfect little church boy," but while I sat smiling in the church pews each Sunday, they knew nothing of the filth within me. No one knew the monster that I was secretly becoming.

Looking back now, I realize there were really two things growing in me. One was wonderful, with the potential for abundant life. But the other was hideous, with the potential for the destruction of myself and many people around me.

This story is not an easy one for me to share since it contains many personal experiences. I will also warn that some of these experiences are not for young ears. While I have tried my best to tell the story without being too graphic, there are experiences in this book that are not healthy for young children.

My hope is that the story of my life will serve as both a warning and a glimmer of hope to others who are struggling silently with sin. A tiny seed of sin can grow up to be a hideous weed that chokes out your life and the lives of those around you. But, the gift that God gives is a relationship with him. This relationship can grow to provide abundant life to everyone it touches.

My desire is that this book would help you see there really is a God in Heaven who loves you and desires a genuine relationship with you. To truly know God is costly, but not nearly as costly as going on without knowing him. And to simply know God is a pleasure greater than every other.

The Early Years

Chapter 1
Innocence Lost

My story has its beginning in a small city located in northeastern Kansas. The year was 1983, and it was a quiet fall evening. My parents and four-year-old sister were temporarily living at my grandparents' house while the construction of their new home was nearing completion.

My parents went to bed that Friday evening thinking about the plans for the next day. The idea was for my dad and some of his friends to move our belongings into our new house. But unbeknownst to my parents, I was going to interrupt their plans.

Early the next morning, my mom started having contractions. My dad left my four-year-old sister with my grandparents as he rushed my mom to the hospital. Later that morning, I made my entrance into the world. My dad stayed with my mom for a little while and then drove to our new house where he and his friends moved in our belongings.

On Monday, my dad brought my mom and I home

The Man Behind the Mask

from the hospital. I was carried into the house where I would live for all my childhood years.

I made my entrance into the world in the powerful and prosperous nation of the United States of America during a time of peace and prosperity. I was born into a prosperous and religious family.

My dad was a hardworking electrical engineer who came from a close-knit family. His parents had owned their own company and were influential people in their small Ohio community.

My mother was an industrious housewife who had been raised on a farm by hardworking parents.

I was blessed. I had both immediate and extended family that truly loved me. My physical needs were always taken care of, and my parents wanted me to learn to love God. Oh, sure, my family was not perfect, even though many at our church thought it was. But in a time when more and more families were falling apart, ours was not.

My life had begun. I had no way of knowing the journey that lay ahead of me, but then, I guess that is what makes life exciting.

This may seem odd, but my earliest memory is of praying a prayer. You have to understand my family was very religious. We did not just go to church on Sunday. If the church doors were open, we were there. If a church function was going on, we attended. And every morning,

Innocence Lost

we learned something from the Bible in our family devotions.

I prayed "the prayer" when I was about four years old. I remember sitting in our living room during our family's morning devotional. My dad asked me if I wanted to ask Jesus into my heart to save me. I do not know if I really understood what I was doing. But I answered, "Yes," and then repeated the prayer after him. My parents told me that Jesus now lived in my heart and I would go to Heaven when I died.

My second childhood memory happened about two years after I said that prayer. It was time for me to start going to school. I really did not want to go. I cried and pleaded with my parents to allow me to stay home, but my dad had decided that it was time. My parents enrolled me in the private Christian school where my sister was already attending.

The only thing I remember about my first day of school is the fire alarm. My fellow kindergartners and I were sitting at our desks coloring pictures when suddenly an ear piercing alarm sounded. Immediately, our teacher lined us all up, marched us upstairs, and walked us out of the building.

Soon, the fire trucks came speeding up and squealed to a stop in front of the school. We all watched excitedly as the firemen ran into the building. I mean, seriously, if this was what kindergarten was all about, then perhaps it was not so bad after all. We were getting to see fire trucks, and better yet, if the building burned down, we would not have

The Man Behind the Mask

to go to school for a while. But, to our disappointment, there was no fire. There was just some dust that set off the smoke alarm. After cleaning the alarm, the firemen headed out, and the excitement was over.

Time went on. I was still a young, ignorant little kid, but I was learning my alphabet and all those other important kindergarten skills, like snack time and using Elmer's glue to glue my hands to my worksheets. I was young and innocent as they say, but then one day something happened that would profoundly impact my life.

My house sat a couple miles outside the city limits, and there was a gravel road that ran next to it. This particular day, my sister and I were walking down the gravel road enjoying the lovely summer weather. We were about a block away from our house, when a man drove up in his car. We looked at him curiously as he pulled up beside us and rolled down his window.

Looking at us in a strange way, he asked for directions. I felt uncomfortable about the way he was looking at us. Something about it seemed wrong. My sister responded that she did not know how to get there.

As my sister was talking, I looked into the car. My young mind started churning as I noticed the man had his pants pulled down. He was rubbing his genitals. I was young and had no idea what was going on, but unknowingly, a seed of curiosity was planted in me.

The man drove off without any physical contact with my sister or me, but this experience would start me down a dangerous path. The effects were subtle at first, but the

Innocence Lost

seed was planted. Eventually, this seed would grow up and almost destroy my life.

Over the next several years, I found myself doing little things without knowing why. One day while I was swimming with my sister, I exposed myself by suddenly pulling my swimming trunks down to my knees. My sister promptly tattled on me. My mom was far from pleased and sent me to my room. I can remember knowing at the time that I should not have done it. I even wondered why I did it. Looking back, I can see my curiosity came from the man my sister and I met on the gravel road.

There were also times when friends would come over and I would find myself doing odd things. I remember once when some kids my age came over to visit. A couple of the girls and I were playing in my room. As we were playing, I lie down on the floor and pulled my shirt up while convincing the girls to play with cars and other toys on my bare stomach.

I also found myself doing many other things while playing by myself. I was fascinated with my body long before I hit puberty or knew the facts of life. I did not realize the experience with the man on the gravel road had placed within me an insatiable curiosity for things I knew nothing about.

My childhood was also filled with a lot of the normal things kids do. Although I was never one to make a lot of friends, I still had plenty of fun.

I really enjoyed time by myself and happily spent many hours outside jumping on my trampoline. While

The Man Behind the Mask

jumping, I would imagine that I was flying through space in a spaceship or sailing the stormy oceans with a band of pirates. I loved windy days when I could jump on the trampoline and feel the wind pushing me through the air.

I spent many days climbing trees or tramping in the pasture behind our house. Even though I was still within eyesight of my house, my imagination carried me to the distant reaches of our galaxy. I knew so little and imagined so much. Life was simple.

When I went to school and started making friends, I can remember always feeling different. I never really fit in with the crowd. I always had a sense of right and wrong and tried to do what was right. This often cost me friends, or at least the approval of my so-called friends.

I can remember one time in particular when I was in second grade. I was invited over to a fellow classmate's house for his birthday party. We ate some cake and then watched a video.

As the video started playing, I realized that it was a TV program that my parents did not want me to watch. I discreetly closed my eyes so I would not see it. I did not want to watch it since I knew my parents had said I could not watch this show. But, I was too embarrassed to tell my friends that my parents did not want me to be watching it. Although they did not know I was not watching the program, it reminded me once again that I was different.

After the show, my friend's mom said we could go outside and play in the woods behind the house as long as we did not go past the fence. My friend led us out into the woods. When we got to the fence, he just kept on going. My friends followed, but I stopped at the fence and waited for them to come back. Although nobody said anything to me, I knew they thought I was stupid for not following along.

When I got home from the birthday party, my parents asked me how it went. I told them about not crossing the fence because my friend's mom had told us not to. After hearing this, my parents took me out for ice cream as a reward for obeying my friend's mom.

Time went by, and I found myself entering third grade. I can remember feeling so grown up as I looked around and saw the kindergarteners and first and second graders. They looked so young. All around me, my friends were growing up.

I led a very sheltered life at home, but some of my friends at school were not so sheltered. They were not teenagers yet, but they were learning about the facts of life. While they did not understand everything, they knew enough to start making lewd jokes.

I was always uncomfortable when they began to tell these jokes. Usually, I would just walk away when they started talking about such things. But my discomfort was obvious to them, and sometimes they laughed at my uneasiness. It never really bothered me when they laughed at me, but it once again made me realize that I was different. I did not fit in with the crowd.

After third grade, my parents decided they were going to homeschool my sister and me. They broke this news to us while we were driving in the car one day. My sister and I listened as Dad told us that he had heard from God. He said God told him that we were supposed to homeschool.

The Man Behind the Mask

Growing up in such a religious family, I was not surprised God had told my parents this, but I was a little unsure as to whether or not I wanted to be homeschooled. My sister, on the other hand, was quite adamant she did not want to be homeschooled. But as always, my parent's decision won out, and the homeschooling began.

Homeschooling was a new concept at this time. Not many people were doing it. My grandparents were quite concerned my sister and I would not get a good education and would miss out on socializing with other kids. But once Dad had his mind set on something, there was no turning around. Homeschooling it was.

There were some rough days as my parents, sister, and I adjusted to learning at home, but overall, I think it went fairly well. I know there were many days when my mom got frustrated. I am sure I did not help things out with my many frustrated outbursts.

Dad helped me with math and the sciences, and mom helped me with my other subjects. I seemed to pick up the math and science pretty well, but I struggled with English. I am amazed my mom did not give up trying to teach me English. I can remember numerous occasions when I let out my frustration and anger on my poor mother. It took me years of going over and over it before I finally started to catch on.

Along with these typical activities of growing up, something else began happening. One day I was playing outside with my friend when I experienced something I would not comprehend until many years down the road.

Innocence Lost

I was about eight years old at the time. It was a beautiful summer day as I looked out over the pasture behind my house. Looking over the landscape, I had this thought that there was something out there. Not that there was something out there in the pasture or up in the sky, but that there was something more to this world than the panorama that met my eyes.

I told my friend that I thought there was something out there. I did not know what it was, but I was certain there was something more than what we could see.

With my friend's suggestion, we headed off to scour the pasture to see what was out there. We spent the afternoon tromping around, with my friend constantly asking if a certain tree, vine, or rock was perhaps what I was talking about.

I finally had to tell him that I still sensed there was something more, but I doubted we would be able to find it by searching the pasture anymore. We gave up our afternoon search, and I promptly forgot about the feeling. I did not realize it at the time, but I had just heard God's voice.

Teen Years

Chapter 2
The Tug of War

While my early years were mostly free of struggle, my teen years found me in a tug of war. At about age twelve, I was entering a dark period of my life. I had a great family, friends, and toys. Yet with all this, something was missing.

It seemed that even with everything I had, there was no real reason to live. I began spiraling down into depression. I would put a smile on the outside and pretend everything was okay, but inside I was withering away.

I got so depressed I did not even want to get out of bed. At night, I would cry myself to sleep. I did not know what was wrong with me. I did not want my parents to find out I was crying, so I would cover my head with my pillow to muffle my cries. After crying for a while, sleep would finally overtake me. And, really, sleep was the only thing I looked forward to each day because I could forget about life for a little while.

Eventually, I did not even want to live anymore. I thought about ways to take my own life. But, I did not follow through because I knew my death would bring pain to my family and friends.

The Man Behind the Mask

After about a year of depression, I searched the Bible for an answer. I found verses that taught about singing praises to God even when times were hard. I began forcing myself to praise and thank God every day. Over the course of about a year of praising and thanking God, the depression slowly disappeared. I still struggled to find a reason to live, but at least the worst of the depression had passed.

Just coming out of depression, I began searching for purpose. My parents were Christians, but I did not want to blindly follow their beliefs. I had to find out for myself if God was real. I determined from that moment that I would not be a fake. If God was real, then I would give him my life. But, if God was a fairy tale, then I would live my life for myself.

I had read in the Bible that if we seek, we will find. So, I decided to put this to the test. I began to spend time each day reading the Bible and asking God to reveal himself to me.

Shortly after this, something happened that really started me on my quest for God. It happened at the church my family attended. On many occasions during Sunday services, the pastor's wife would give "words" to people. These were specific words that she and others (and now myself) believed were things God told her to share with the congregation. Many times these were very specific words for individual people.

This particular Sunday morning, she had a "word" for me. She told me to "Seek God to hear." I hastily jotted this

The Tug of War

down on a scrap of paper and tucked it away. Looking at it later, I wondered what exactly it meant. I was already seeking God, but I did not really understand what I was supposed to hear.

Not long after I received this "word," I began to notice other people talking about hearing God speak to them. I knew others claimed to hear God speak, but I did not have a clue as to how they heard or what God sounded like. I had read in the Bible about many times when people heard God speak, but the questions remained: Did God really speak? And, if he did, does he still speak today?

This really marked the beginning of my search for God and my desire to know if God still speaks. From my recent experience with depression, I already realized possessions would never satisfy me. I had to have something real.

I did not know how to interact with God, but I began to try. Sometimes I would spend hours just sitting in my room waiting. I would say, "God, are you there?" But I never heard a response.

I also tried reading my Bible. While the Bible stories seemed good, I was after more. I did not want to just read about God. I needed to know if he was actually real. Did he really have a mouth and ears like the Bible said, or was the Bible just full of fairy tales?

It was during this time of seeking in my early teen years that I first knowingly experienced the "presence of God." Our church was having regular prayer times after the Sunday and Wednesday church services. These were times when people could come up to the front of the church and spend time praying. I was seeking for something real and came up regularly during these times. On one of these occasions, a guy from our church came to me and asked if I had ever felt the presence of God.

I replied that I did not really know. He asked me if I wanted to. Replying that I did, he asked me to raise my hands. As I did, he put his hands a few inches away from mine.

I immediately felt something in my hands, and then it flooded my whole body. The feeling is hard to describe, but it felt like being blanketed with peace and experiencing the satisfying of a deep longing. It was like experiencing the deepest longing of my heart being satisfied without the longing going away. I compare it to being hungry while eating. The hunger is not a bad thing while you are eating. It simply allows you to eat. The presence of God was like that, feeling a deep longing while having the longing satisfied at the same time.

This taste of God's presence was what I had been looking for. I had found something that satisfied, and I began throwing myself into seeking the presence of God. Many days I would spend hours in prayer. Sometimes I would go for days or even weeks without feeling God's presence, but the moments I experienced it made the waiting worth it. To experience God became my reason to live. It was a pleasure that fulfilled, and it did not matter how many hours of seeking it took. A minute in his presence was life itself.

I began trying to figure out a set of steps that would always bring me into God's presence. I tried reading the Bible, praying, singing, and doing other things. When something brought me into the tangible presence of God, I

The Tug of War

would try doing the exact same thing the next day. But it seemed like the same thing never worked two days in a row. I was frustrated for a while, but eventually I learned that God is not into formulas. He is much more into relationships. If he had allowed the same set of steps to always work, I would have forgotten about him and just gone through the steps to "feel good."

There were many times while I was spending time in God's presence that thoughts would come into my mind. These thoughts were different than the thousands of regular thoughts I had every day. Whenever these thoughts came, they came with a gentle force and seemed to resonate within me. I did not realize it at the time, but I was beginning to hear God's voice.

Around this same time, my dad and I went on a backpacking trip. It was on the drive home from this trip that my dad gave me "the birds and the bees" talk. I remember feeling awkward as I listened to my dad talk. My eyes stared straight ahead at the passing scenery as the facts of life were unfolded to me. It all sounded kind of disgusting at the time. I mean, seriously, what was God thinking when he thought this up!

While all this newfound knowledge seemed a bit gross, it immediately reawakened the curiosity in me. This curiosity had been building subconsciously in me ever since the man on the gravel road had asked for directions. And now it came pounding at my door.

I quickly developed an insatiable desire to know what the female body looked like, not just a diagram in an

The Man Behind the Mask

encyclopedia, but a real photo. I knew it was wrong, but the desire kept growing.

Finally, my curiosity got the best of me. I was home alone for a little while and decided to find a photo on the Internet. I justified it by telling myself that I would only take one look to see what a woman looked like.

I nervously crept into my dad's office and quietly closed the door behind me. Hurrying over to his computer, I opened the Internet and did a search for some very descriptive words. An endless list of websites showed up.

My heart pounded in my chest as I clicked the link to the first site. I was surprised as a warning page appeared. The message asked me to click the box to verify I was eighteen years old or older. With my strong moral upbringing, I could not bring myself to lie about my age. I went to the next site but was disappointed to find the same age verification required.

After finding the same warning on several sites, my curiosity overtook my better judgment. I clicked the box indicating that I was eighteen years old. Suddenly the porn site flashed before my eyes. The screen was filled with numerous little photos of women that could be clicked on to enlarge. I hesitated for a moment as I listened to make sure my parents were not returning.

Hearing nothing, my eyes darted back to the computer screen as I clicked on a photo. The image enlarged before my eyes, and I found myself peering at a woman's body. But, it did not show the details I was looking for. I opened another photo and then another and another. Before I knew what had happened, I had seen numerous revealing photos and had a sensual experience like nothing I had ever experienced before.

The Tug of War

I was immediately filled with guilt. But at the same time, I enjoyed the pleasure that resulted from looking at these photos. It did not take long for me to develop a habit of looking at photos of women online, in magazines, and in catalogs. I could not get enough of it.

Around this time, my parents purchased a used minivan. I was riding in the minivan one day when I noticed something under one of the seats. Pulling it out, I realized it was an XXX rated porn movie. My parents did not know it, but the previous owners had accidentally left the movie in the van.

The next time I found myself home alone, I placed the video in the VCR and turned it on. I was shocked at what I saw. Women were doing unthinkable things with other women. Then men and women were doing things together. They were performing acts far beyond the natural use of sex. I knew what I was seeing was incredibly wrong, but my thirst for a deeper sensual experience had me like a fish on a hook. And I was getting helplessly reeled in. When I finished watching the video, I carefully hid it back in the van.

A few months later, the previous owners contacted my parents and told them they had left the video in the van. They said they did not want it back. My parents found the video and threw it into the garbage.

When I discovered my parents had thrown the video away, I rummaged through the foul-smelling garbage and retrieved the video. After cleaning off the case, I placed it into the VCR again and turned it on. Part way through the video my spirit became so agitated that I finally decided to stop watching it and threw it back into the garbage.

Along with looking at pornography, I started

The Man Behind the Mask

masturbating. It started as just every now and then but quickly grew to consume much of my time. Soon it became an addiction.

Sadly, the hours a day that I had been using for seeking God in prayer and reading the Bible began to be consumed by looking at pornography and masturbating.

After a few years, it got to the point where I would masturbate multiple times almost every day. I was addicted to these momentary sensual experiences. My body craved the pleasure, but at the same time, I always knew it would not satisfy. There would be the moment of pleasure, but it was always followed by the disappointment and the wish that I had never done it. It left me physically and emotionally drained and filled with shame. I felt like a captive animal chained to my addiction.

My addiction became my reason for living. Almost everything I did and everywhere I went became an opportunity for some sexual fantasy. One summer vacation found me doing something that could have gotten me into serious trouble.

My family and I were camping at a campground in Arkansas that summer. At one point, I was left alone at our campsite while the rest of my family went to the camp showers. The showers were located at the far end of the campsite, so I knew I would have some time before my family returned.

I had been making a plan, and now seemed like the best time to execute it. While using the camp bathroom the day before, I noticed the dividing wall between the men's

The Tug of War

and women's side did not go all the way to the ceiling. And I noticed a possible way to climb up one of the stalls.

The time was now or never. I nervously looked around to make sure that my family was out of sight. Seeing no sign of them, I began walking quickly to the nearby campground bathroom.

Nearing the bathroom, I slowed my pace and glanced around to make sure no one was coming. Seeing no one, I slipped inside the men's side.

I proceeded to carefully climb up the stall. As I neared the top, I reached one hand over the edge. For a brief minute, I began to think about what I was doing. My conscience started pleading with me to stop, but my body was craving yet another sensual experience. With my conscience still pleading, I placed both my hands on the top of the wall and slowly pulled.

Pulling myself quietly to the top, I cautiously poked my head over the wall. Looking down, I could see straight into the women's stalls. My eyes peered quickly from one stall to the next, but each one was empty. It turned out there were no women using the bathroom at the time. Part of me was disappointed, but part of me was relieved. I carefully climbed back down and walked back to our tent.

As I waited for my family to return, I started to comprehend exactly what I had done. I realized my sexual addictions were pushing me to do things I would never have dreamed of doing.

As time went on, the addictions grew. What I had done yesterday was never enough. The need for something more real was constantly in my face. I started looking at lingerie catalogs before I went to bed to help fuel my dreams at night.

At one point, my dreams took on a life of their own. Somehow I had come to the point where I would periodically become conscious of the fact that I was dreaming while I was still asleep. When this would occur, I found that I could control what I did in my dreams to some extent. During these dreams, I would do unspeakably detestable things to women. When I awoke from these dreams, I would be shocked at what I had done. But at the same time, I wanted to do it again.

Eventually it got to the point where it was not enough to just do it in my dreams. I began to fantasize horrible things when I was around women. Many times when I saw them, I would get strong impulses to rape them or do other appalling things to them. Without realizing it, I had come to the point where I no longer saw women as people, but simply as objects for pleasure.

I saw a lady one day, and the impulse to rape her became extremely strong. It actually scared me. I literally had to hold myself back from jumping on her.

At this point, I realized I needed help. I saw that the little seeds that had been planted years ago had sprouted and grown into a hideous plant that I was unable to deal with. My earlier decision to disobey God by "just taking one look" had come back to haunt me. I was scared, but I did not know what to do to get free.

After this scare, I resolved to stop masturbating and looking at pornography. For the most part, I was able to stop looking at pornography. But I could not seem to stop masturbating. I tried to stop numerous times, but the best I could manage was about a week before I would once again

The Tug of War

succumb to the haunting desire.

One time during a vacation, I was able to go a week without masturbating. After getting home from vacation, I tried to keep the desire at bay. It was excruciatingly difficult, but I managed to stop for a second consecutive week. But after these two weeks, the desire overpowered me again. I fell right back into my addiction. I was miserable. Everything in me longed for the momentary pleasure, but at the same time, I was sick of it and desperately wanted to be free. I realized that there was no way I could quit masturbating on my own. I was a caged animal.

It was at this time that God miraculously delivered me. It was my senior year of high school, and I was still homeschooling. While doing school work at my desk one day, I got the urge to masturbate. I was about to give in, when I suddenly heard God say, "Stop it." I was shocked that God would tell me this because I figured he knew how desperately I wanted to stop but how unable I was to quit. Getting up from my desk, I walked to my room.

Kneeling down at my bed, I told God there was no way I could stop in my own strength. I told him I would stop if he gave me the ability to. And just like that, God set me free. I only had a faint desire to masturbate the next couple of days, and then the desire was completely gone. From time to time, the desire would come back, but never with the tremendous force that it had before. I was always able to easily ignore it. This deliverance helped me realize that God has power and can act in our lives.

While I never fell back into masturbating or looking at pornography, the effects still lingered on for several years. From time to time, the pornography images would come up in my mind, and sensual desires still arose whenever I was around women. It took me five years at college before the effects began fading away.

By the time I graduated college, my past addictions were just fading memories. I still struggled with lust, but I figured it was only to the same degree that many men in our society do.

God would do an incredible cleansing in me about five years after I graduated from college. But for now, that would have to wait.

Chapter 3
Spiritual Growth

Even during the years that I found myself chained to addictions, I was still seeking after God. But it was a continuous tug of war. On the one hand, I was falling deeper and deeper into darkness. On the other hand, I was still searching for a God that was real.

I was searching because I had to know if God was real, and if he was real, whether or not he was worth following. I had many experiences during my teen years that slowly brought me to the point of acknowledging there really was a God who was worth following.

I just related my experience of God delivering me from the addiction, but he had already delivered me from something else before that. This "something" was anger.

This deliverance happened around the same time I first knowingly experienced the presence of God and was beginning to hear God speak.

At the time, my parents had been homeschooling my sister and me for a few years. And naturally, there were times of friction between us.

Being both a parent and a teacher has to be hard, and I

The Man Behind the Mask

admire my parents for hanging in there all those years. While they did well teaching my sister and me, there were definitely times of friction.

Sometimes I simply did not want to do school at all. At other times, my personality clashed with mom's teaching style. There were plenty of times throughout our homeschooling days when family friction arose.

Sometimes I would get angry. But I usually kept my thoughts to myself. People around me had no idea the extent to which the anger was boiling inside me. I am sure my parents could see the tip of the iceberg, but they did not realize how much anger I was holding in.

One day, as the anger welled up inside of me, I sensed God telling me to let go of it. But I was unable to let go of it in my own strength. I tried for a while, but the anger just came. There did not seem to be anything I could do about it.

Finally, I told God that I would give up my anger. But it would require him setting me free because I could not do it on my own. Amazingly, the anger toward my mom left me that very day and never returned.

I began to think about the possibility that God was really speaking to me and that he had actually set me free from anger. I was still not sure about this hearing God thing, but this experience did get me thinking.

As I continued to seek God, I began experiencing something that I initially relegated to coincidence. During my frequent prayer times, God would share various things with me. Then, oddly enough, I would go to church the

Spiritual Growth

next Sunday only to hear Pastor preach about the same thing God had been telling me that very week. Many times the message would be from the exact same passage of scripture that God had been teaching me about.

At first I considered this a coincidence, but eventually, I came to grips with the fact that it was something more when it continued to happen every week for several months.

I was still not sold on the idea that God was really speaking to me, but I was starting to think seriously about it now.

As my high school years approached, my dad told me that I needed to get a job. He said I could get a job somewhere or he would be happy to help me start a business. We thought about different ideas and finally decided on starting a lawn mower repair and tune-up business.

I created some advertisement fliers in order to get the business started. Early that spring, my dad and I walked around the nearby neighborhoods putting fliers on people's doors.

We also made a couple yard signs for additional advertisement. One sign was placed in the yard of a friend who lived in town, and the other sign was put in our yard. The fliers and signs worked, and soon people were calling me about getting their mowers tuned up and repaired.

As we started to get business, my dad taught me the basics of small engine repair. He continued to help me for the first couple of years as I learned how to repair the mowers. From that point on, I learned through my own experience.

Due to my low overhead costs, I was able to provide extremely competitive pricing. I was also careful to schedule the repairs so that I was able to complete them within a week or less. This was much better than the several weeks that other repair shops usually took.

The competitive pricing and honest, reliable service resulted in many satisfied customers who continued to return the following years. In fact, even after I went to college, I continued to get calls from repeat customers who wanted to have their mowers tuned up. I continued to take some repeat business for the first couple of summers during college, but eventually had to turn requests down as I became busy with other jobs.

Overall, the business turned out to be a great job through my high school years. This work provided me with the opportunity to learn about mower repair and also how to run a customer-oriented business.

Not only did I learn how to repair mowers and run a business, but I also had an unexpected opportunity to learn about recognizing God's voice again. This happened as I was trying to repair a lawn mower that I could not get to run correctly. The engine would barely start, and then it would die after choking for a few seconds. I have learned more about engine repair since then, but at the time, I was convinced it was an electrical problem. I tried everything I could think of, but nothing would get it to run correctly. I was determined to fix it, but I had run out of ideas to try.

Out of desperation, I finally decided to take this to God. I went into my room and told God that I was going to pray until he told me what to do to fix the mower. I had

Spiritual Growth

been praying for about ten minutes when the thought came to me that I should clean out the carburetor.

At the time, I did not have the understanding I do now. The solution of cleaning out the carburetor seemed like a ludicrous idea. I did not think there was any way this would fix the problem. To be honest, I began thinking maybe I had not been hearing from God all along since this latest idea was clearly wrong. I decided I would give it a try just to prove this was not really God.

I headed back outside and proceeded to take apart the carburetor. After cleaning and rebuilding the carburetor, I put the mower back together and pulled the starter rope. To my utter amazement, the engine kicked to life and continued to run fine.

I must say this made me take a step back and think seriously about the fact that perhaps God really was speaking. I had no idea how to fix this mower, and God told me what to do. Crazy as it sounded, I was hearing from God.

College Days

Chapter 4
The Shock

Time passed on. I graduated from high school and entered the next phase of my life. Over the last few years, I had been coming to the conclusion that God was real and was actually speaking to me. So, during the last year of high school, I had been asking God where I should go to college. I prayed a lot about it but did not hear any response.

During this time, my family and I visited various colleges, but none of them seemed right. I kept praying about it but was not hearing anything.

I am the type who likes to plan ahead, and things were getting uncomfortably down to the wire. None of the colleges we visited seemed right. And God did not seem to be saying anything. With all the uncertainty, I was growing nervous.

The Man Behind the Mask

With only a few months before the fall semester would begin, my dad got the idea of visiting the University of Missouri Rolla (UMR). When we returned from this visit, God told me clearly this was where I was supposed to go. I had never felt such assurance that I had heard from God. But when I told my parents that I felt God wanted me to go to UMR, they said they would not allow me to go to UMR unless I could get different housing. We had toured the dorms on our campus visit, and they were not pleased with the fact that there were pornographic posters in the dorm hallways. My parents did not want me living in that environment.

The problem was UMR required students to live in campus housing for the first two years. My dad tried to get them to waive this requirement and allow me to live in an off-campus apartment. But the college would not budge. It was looking like my only option for housing was in the dorms, but this would mean going against my parents' wishes.

I was very confused. On the one hand, I had never been so sure of God's direction, but on the other hand, the Bible stated we are to honor our parents.

So, once again, I put God to the test. I told God if this was really where he wanted me to go, then he would have to make a way for me to go to UMR *with* my parents' blessing.

Well, God came through. With less than three months before the beginning of the semester, UMR let us know they were starting a "Holistic Community" on one floor of the dorms. It would be a floor where a lot of junk (including raunchy pictures) would not be allowed. I must say I just about exploded when I heard the news. I was

The Shock

once again confronted with the fact that not only was God speaking, but he could intervene in my life. It was off to college for me.

Wow, was college ever a shock to my system! As I mentioned earlier, I was raised in a sheltered home. Oh sure, I had heard sin abounded in the world and had experienced plenty myself. But I guess I did not realize both the extent and openness of sin in society. My first semester proved to be a real eye opener.

I arrived at college for orientation week, and all of us freshmen were divided into small groups led by various upperclassmen. These groups met periodically and went to several planned events to get us familiar with the campus and college life.

In my group's first meeting, the leader asked everyone to tell their name, their hometown, and what kind of music they liked. We went around the circle with everyone naming music that I had either never heard of or knew was immoral. When it was my turn, I said I liked contemporary Christian music. No one said anything, but it was clear I was the only one who listened to Christian music. It brought back memories of feeling different back in my Christian school days. Once again, I did not fit in with the crowd.

Orientation week came to a close and classes began. This was when the real shock came. I could not believe the conversations people had and the language they used. Everywhere I went, I heard people cussing and talking about sexual topics that I would have never dreamed of

The Man Behind the Mask

discussing openly.

In fact, during one of my first Introduction to Engineering classes, the teacher told a lewd joke. It seemed like everywhere I went, sex was talked about, joked about, and described in far more detail than I care to mention.

Although I was not there at the time, one of my friends who worked for the campus police related a story about a girl in one of the dorms. While wearing only a robe, she had walked down to the boy's floor and proceeded to slip off the robe and walk stark naked down the boy's hallway!

Another time, I overheard a conversation that broke my heart. I was working with my chemistry lab partner on an experiment when I was surprised by the conversation a couple of girls were having. The one girl began talking about how she had been sleeping around with some guys. Again, I was shocked at how open people were about sex. I was surprised she would just casually talk about this where my lab partner and I could hear. I was curious, so I paused what I was doing and listened.

She went on to say she had just slept with a guy and was lamenting about it. I could sense her brokenness as she went on to say she wished she never had sex.

After the chemistry lab was over, I thought about the girls' conversation as I walked back to my dorm room. My heart was broken for this girl, and my mind was still in a state of shock at the openness of these girls' conversation.

On yet another occasion, I was once again stunned by some students' conversation. I had arrived early to class and was sitting at a desk waiting for the class to begin. The professor had not arrived yet, and there were a few guys and girls sitting around me.

The Shock

As I sat there, a few of the guys started talking about what they had done the previous weekend. They talked about the women at a bar they had gone to. Before long, they were talking in detail about the women and making lewd jokes about the women's bodies. I was repulsed. It was obvious some of the girls in the class did not appreciate what they were saying, but no one did anything. I felt like standing up and telling these guys to shut up, but I was too afraid. I did not appreciate their disrespect for women, but I had no place to point fingers.

It was not just the openness of other students' conversations that shocked me. It was the openness of their lives.

One particular event happened on a Saturday morning. I had slept in until the middle of the morning as I usually did on Saturdays and was getting ready for the day. Sitting there in my dorm room, I grabbed a bite to eat and thought about the homework that I had to get done.

After eating, I slipped on my shower shoes, grabbed my toothbrush, and headed to the dorm bathroom. Feeling the steam from the showers, I walked over to the sink. I heard a guy's voice coming from the shower area but did not think anything about it.

I had been brushing my teeth for a few seconds when I heard a girl giggling. I froze for a second as my mind registered what was going on. Paralyzed in front of the sink, I heard the guy speak again and heard the girl respond. My heart pounded in my chest as I realized that there was a guy and girl showering together in a shower

The Man Behind the Mask

stall only a few yards from where I stood.

I quickly rinsed out my mouth as a cascade of sensual emotions and uneasiness flooded me. With my mouth rinsed, I speedily made my exit from the restroom and walked briskly back to my room.

Sitting down on my bed, I sat in a state of shock as the last few minutes replayed in my mind. I was astonished at the openness of people's sex lives.

Along with being exposed to the other student's sex lives, there were other obvious differences that made me realize I did not fit in.

Some of my classmates would invite friends to their dorm room to watch a movie. Sometimes these movies were clean, but many times the movies had content I did not want to expose myself to. I always found out what movie they were going to watch before I accepted their invitation.

If the movie was not something I wanted to expose myself to, I would decline the offer. But it was always difficult to say no to my friends. I certainly was not new to peer pressure, but I was embarrassed to tell them that I would not be coming. And even more embarrassed when they began asking why I was not coming. I hated explaining that I did not want to watch a movie because of the content.

While I was typically careful of what I watched, there was one time I bowed to peer pressure. One of my friends invited me and another friend over to watch a movie. I did not even ask what the movie was because this friend

The Shock

typically had good taste.

Arriving at my friend's dorm room, we sat down and started the movie. The movie started out okay, but there was some questionable content as it went on. I was uncomfortable, but I told myself that it was probably just this one scene. Since my friend was watching it, I did not want to make a scene and say I had to leave.

As the movie progressed, the scenes became progressively more sexually graphic. I became more and more uncomfortable, but I was petrified by what my friend would think if I got up and left. At the same time, I knew I should not be letting peer pressure direct my decisions, and this made me all the more uncomfortable.

Finally, the movie became so graphic my friend turned it off and apologized. He had not checked the movie rating and did not know there was graphic content.

I left that evening disappointed in myself for not speaking up sooner. I had made this stand before, but somehow I allowed my friend's opinion to sway me. I asked God for forgiveness and the strength to say no in the future.

Along with not watching certain movies, there was another decision that made me realize I did not fit in with the crowd. I found out that it was pretty much a given that you would make illegal copies of computer games and movies as a student on the college campus.

This pirating of computer games and movies was so rampant that there were file sharing sites set up for this very purpose. I was surprised to find out that even many of

The Man Behind the Mask

my Christian friends were involved with pirating. They did not seem to think twice about it. It was just what you did.

There were a few multi-player games that my friends enjoyed playing. They asked me if they could copy one onto my computer so I could play with them. When they asked, I was stunned. Not wanting to make a scene, I let them do it. But later, I bought the game so it would be legal.

Overall, I was continuously bombarded by these things that made me constantly aware I did not fit in with the crowd. I did not want to be a "goody two shoes" as one of my classmates called me. And, I did not want to make a scene. I simply did not want to do what I knew was wrong.

Chapter 5
Still in God's Hands

I made a commitment when I started college. I committed to continuing spending about thirty minutes in prayer each morning no matter the circumstances. I expected life to get busy, and I did not want to neglect what was most important.

While it was difficult many mornings, I always forced myself out of bed and into the shower to wake myself up. After showering, I would have a prayer time in my room if my roommate was not there. If my roommate was there, I went to one of the private study rooms at the campus library.

Although there were many distractions throughout my college days, these times of prayer each morning helped keep me steady.

During my first semester, I was constantly aware of the sin and brokenness in the people around me. I wanted to do something for them, but I did not know what to do. I wanted to share Jesus with them, but I was still questioning my own faith and did not know what to say to them.

Not knowing what else to do, I started prayer walking around campus. Many evenings found me walking the campus sidewalks asking God to break through into these people's lives.

I had also been going to the weekly Campus Christian Fellowship (CCF) meetings that were held on campus. At one particular CCF meeting, one of the members announced he would be leading a prayer time after the evening meeting. He asked anyone interested to meet him in the middle of campus at the "Puck." The Puck was a round, concrete platform in the center of campus that was used for various outdoor campus events.

I met up with him after the meeting, and we headed over to the Puck. There was no one at the Puck when we arrived, so we waited. After a few minutes, we realized it was just going to be the two of us. We were disappointed no one else showed up for prayer, but it gave us a chance to get to know each other a little better. It was nice to talk to someone else who also wanted people to know God. After talking for a while, we ended up having a great prayer time and then parted ways for the evening.

While my first semester crawled by slowly, time started flying once my second semester hit. Before I knew it, I was already coming to the end of my second year of college.

I began looking for a job that I could do over the summer. UMR did a lot to help students get internships.

Still in God's Hands

So, I entered my resume to see if I could get one.

While I was waiting to see if any companies would contact me, I asked God what I should do for the summer. I sensed God wanted me to work for Dave, a guy from my church back home. He had his own construction site cleanup business and had hired several people from our church over the years. I decided I would go home on my next three-day weekend and ask Dave for a job.

Not long before my next trip home, I was contacted by a company that thought I would be a good fit for an internship. I was interested in robotics, and this company did work in the automation field. The company told me that I could have a couple of weeks to decide if I wanted to pursue their offer.

Here I was with what seemed like an excellent opportunity for an internship, but with a sense God wanted me to do some dirty, hard labor. I decided I would ask Dave for a job. If he said yes, then I would go ahead and do that. But if he said no, then I would pursue the internship opportunity.

Soon the three-day weekend arrived, and I headed home. That Sunday I approached Dave about a job. Now, you have to understand, I had always been very self-conscious and lacked confidence in myself. So just the idea of asking Dave for a job made me really nervous.

I timidly approached Dave and asked if I could work for him over the summer. Looking at my scrawny build, Dave warned me in his direct manner that it would be hard, dirty labor and he could only employ me part time. But he would let me work for him if I wanted to. I replied that I wanted to and that I would contact him when my semester was over.

The Man Behind the Mask

With a summer job secured, I headed back to finish my school semester. I had no way of knowing God was going to use this job to build a friendship that I desperately needed.

Now that I had my summer plans sealed, I called the company that had been interested in me and told them I already had another job lined up for the summer. As I hung up the phone, my mind wandered. I was glad I would be home for the summer, but I wondered if I had missed a great opportunity.

Soon my second year of college was over, and I headed home for summer break. When I got home, I told Dave that I was ready to start work, and he let me know what time to show up for my first day.

The day arrived, and I drove up and parked beside the beat up old van that would take me to the first job site. As I mentioned earlier, I was a bit timid. And I was not physically that strong. Although I did a lot of running and biking, my upper body had not received much attention. I was far more of a bookworm than a laborer, and I had no idea what God had gotten me into.

As I arrived, Dave and his son met me. They were both wearing shorts and t-shirts. Looking at the jeans I was wearing, Dave told me bluntly I was probably going to get too hot.

With that, Dave handed me a pair of cheap work gloves and climbed into the van's driver seat. He motioned for me to get in. I started to climb into the front passenger seat but noticed there was already a large plastic alien sitting there. Looking over, his son dryly informed me that I would have to sit on the wooden chair in the back of the van because the front seat belonged to the alien. I realized I

Still in God's Hands

was in for an interesting summer.

Climbing into the back of the van, I looked at my "seat." It was a wooden chair that looked like it had once belonged at a kitchen table but now would be more suited for the dump. But it was better than standing, at least a little better.

Once I sat down, Dave turned the key in the ignition and pumped the gas pedal, and the van slowly sputtered to life. We pulled out of the driveway with his son following us in an old green pickup truck that was fondly dubbed "The Green Machine." With that, we were on our way to my first job.

Arriving at the first house, my job was to scrape the plywood floors in an almost completed house to prepare it for the flooring to be laid. Dave gave me a five-second demonstration of what I was to do and then handed me a long-handled scraper. The three of us spent a few hours scraping the floors. By the time we were finished, I was hot and tired, and my hands were beginning to blister.

With the first house completed, we climbed back in the van and headed to our second job for the day. This job was to pick up the construction trash from another house that was being built. We spent the afternoon picking up the trash and putting it into the Green Machine.

By the end of the first day, I was filthy and exhausted. My scrawny, one hundred thirty-pound frame was not accustomed to this hard labor, and every part of my body ached. And, it was only day one.

The summer continued on, and the days turned into weeks and the weeks into months. Most of our jobs consisted of what we did best: pick stuff up and put it in the truck. The hard labor and hot sun did wonders for me. I

The Man Behind the Mask

was soon well tanned and had gained over fifteen pounds of muscle. Though the work was filthy and physically exhausting, I really enjoyed it for the most part. Dave, his son, and I were always talking, joking, and playing tricks on each other.

There was always fun to be had. Sometimes it was finding a panel of shiny solar board and quietly aiming it just right so the sun reflected onto the back of one of the other guys. It was amazing how much heat the solar board directed, and before long, they would be sweating profusely before realizing what was going on. Of course, once you had fried someone with solar board, you had to be on the watch-out for the possibility of retaliation in the form of a flying two-by-four or other construction debris.

The summer flew by, and I found myself getting ready to return to college for the fall semester. Looking back, I am so glad I obeyed God and worked for Dave. The job had given me an opportunity to develop a close friendship with Dave and his family. While I had gone to church with them for many years, I had never had the opportunity to really develop a friendship with them. Their family was completely opposite from mine, and God used them to help me in a number of ways.

Growing up, my dad had always kept a tight rein on me and was always driving me to perfection. I was never given the opportunity to fail, and I became very self-conscious and terrified to try anything because I was afraid I might fail. I am so thankful for my parents and all that they did. But just like any parents, they were not perfect.

God used my relationship with Dave to grow me up. Dave and his family were very direct. They did not care what anyone else was thinking, and they always let you

Still in God's Hands

know what was on their mind.

As I hung out with them, I slowly learned to just be myself. I was amazed at how relaxing it was to not worry about what they thought about me. To this day, Dave and his wife are like a second set of parents. I am so thankful for how God used them to impact my life.

As my college days were coming to a close, I had an experience that revolutionized my walk with God. For years I had been seeking God and trying to serve him. I knew in my mind that I could not earn my salvation, and I had read in the Bible that Jesus paid for my sins. But somehow this knowledge had not made its way to my heart.

Throughout my life, I had done many good things, but all the while I had been subconsciously trying to earn my salvation. Whenever I helped people, there was always this nagging in the back of my mind reminding me that I was just doing it to ease my own conscience rather than doing it out of love for the individuals.

For years, I was haunted by the thirteenth chapter of First Corinthians. Basically it says we can do anything, even to the extent of giving our bodies to be burned. But our actions are of no benefit if we do not have love. Later in the passage it explains what love is. One aspect of love is that it does not seek its own. All these years, I had done many good things, but only to ease my own conscious (in other words, seeking my own).

During my last year of college, God told me to do some things that I was not able to do in my own strength. I tried to obey but did not have the courage to step out. The more evident my own weaknesses became, the more discouraged I became. I began to feel like I was not good enough for God. In my discouragement, I wrote the following Journal entry:

September 9, 2006 – Well, I don't quite know where this is going to go, but I guess time will tell. I just want to be honest, and yet I question my own ability to be honest with myself. It seems like even if I knew I was wrong, I would hide it from myself and never even know it. Hmmm, that seems a little strange, but I suppose it could be true.

I know there is a God, at least I think I do. I know he has impacted my life, at least I think he has. Why is it that we fear to question God? Is he not big enough to represent himself?

I feel like I could never be good enough to be considered God's. I see my successes and what God has done in my life, but somehow my failures seem to overwhelm me. Can God really love someone as wretched as me? Yes, I know he can. Or do I? I tell myself I know it, but do I really know it? To even question this seems to bring a wave of guilt. What would my parents and other Christians think if they found out I question God from time to time? And yet I wonder if the reason for their reaction would actually be because they, too, have questioned and are afraid to admit it.

But then it comes over me again. I know for certain there is a God. I know he loves me. I just wonder if my name is written in his Book of Life. I just don't know . . . Yes, I do . . . Or, is it just my brain telling me that I know?

Still in God's Hands

God, I know you are real and you have saved me. Well, to be honest, God, I know you are real, but I question the fact that you have saved me. I feel disobedient, and yet I don't know why. I mean, I know I have disobeyed before, but I also know I have obeyed you many times as well. So why do I feel so alone? Where are you, God? I don't hate you. I don't think you are cruel. I know you love me. I know you want me to be saved. I know you want to be with me. Yes, I really know all these things. I absolutely positively know these things.

So what is the question? What am I asking? I guess it all boils down to this: God, I don't think I am obedient enough for you to save me. I fear I am not willing to give you my all. I fear I just can't be obedient enough for you. I need to hear you, God. I've heard you speak many times before. You have set me free from so many things. And yet, there is always this question nagging. Am I really saved? Oh God, please tell me. Please let me know the truth. I really want to be with You . . . forever . . .

My failures were really discouraging me. And as time went on, I became more and more aware of my own inability to obey God in my own strength. Finally I realized that my best was just not good enough. This realization made me miserable.

Trudging slowly up the stairs to my dorm room, I flopped down on my bed. Dejectedly, I told God I loved him and really wanted to continue my relationship with him, but I was not good enough. I told him that I was not going to be a fake, and I was done trying to be good enough.

It broke my heart as I told him our relationship was

over. I realized both the immediate and eternal results of what I was saying, but I was not going to play games with God. I had determined from the moment I started seeking God that I would not be a fake. So this realization of my own inability left me with no other choice than to say good-bye.

No sooner had these words left my mouth, then God tenderly replied, "But I still love you." These words shocked me. Thoughts whirled through my head. How could he love me when it was so evident I could not follow where he was leading? But, as the reality of God's unconditional love settled in, joy flooded my heart. Within a matter of seconds, I went from the lowest point to the best moment of my life. I was overcome with his love.

This event marked a change in my life. After experiencing God's unconditional love, I was able to help others because I wanted to help them. I served others because I loved them, not because I was proving my own goodness. For the first time in my life, I was actually able to help others without seeking my own. Truly God can bring about tremendous change by merely speaking a few words.

Young Adult Years

Chapter 6
Living

Time marched on, and I found myself graduating from college. After graduation, I obtained a full-time position as a mechanical engineer in my hometown. I quickly got into the daily routine of the work schedule.

During this time, God told me to begin going to the International House of Prayer (IHOP). This is a ministry that, among other things, has a building where prayer and worship are going on twenty-four hours a day, seven days a week. Worship bands play there non-stop. The band normally starts playing a song and sings the song for ten or fifteen minutes. Sometimes a single song will last even longer than that.

On one particular day, I was sitting in the prayer room as I randomly opened my Bible. I am not one to normally just open my Bible randomly and start reading, but this particular day I did. I happened to open to the passage about John the Baptist preparing the way for God.

As soon as I got to this passage, the worship team began to sing a song about preparing the way for God. I found this interesting but was not especially amazed. After

The Man Behind the Mask

less than a minute, I finished reading the verses about John the Baptist preparing the way. Suddenly the band abruptly changed songs. I was shocked. I have spent a lot of time at IHOP and rarely does the band ever stop abruptly and move onto another song. On top of that, there has never been another time while I was there when they sang a song for less than a minute or two.

I was amazed at the "coincidence" of how God had set things up. Here I had just randomly opened my Bible to this verse, and the band happened to play this song, play it for just the right amount of time, and abruptly stop playing instead of making a smooth transition to another song. I learned enough statistics in college to know the probability of all these things happening randomly like this was practically impossible.

With all this, I started paying more attention to what I was reading. I read how all the people were asking John the Baptist what they should do to prepare for the coming of Jesus. So I asked God what I should be doing in my life. God immediately replied, "Do what you are doing, and all the more." As soon as I heard those words, I understood what they meant. I had been spending more time in prayer and outreach since graduating from college, and God wanted me to continue doing these things. And to continue to do them more as time went on.

As I continued seeking God, he continued to speak. Most of the things God had asked me to do up to this point were things I wanted to do or things that I could do without other people knowing what I was doing. But, as I got it

Living

settled in my heart that he was really speaking to me, God began to ask greater things.

The first "major" thing God asked me to do was to start leading a prayer time at church. This was a huge step for me in two ways. First, it was always hard for me to take any kind of leadership role. And second, God asked me to play the piano during these prayer times. To me, this was huge since I was extremely nervous about playing the piano in front of people.

I spent a lot of time in prayer, making sure this was really what God wanted me to do. God would not let it go as I wrestled with this for several months. The more I prayed about it, the more I realized I actually desired to lead the prayer time.

Even though I wanted to do this, I still struggled to get the courage to step out and do it. As I continued praying, God told me that I did not have to do it but that he wanted me to do it. I understood God would be saddened if I did not do it. It was at this point that I said, "Okay."

I was really scared, but my desire to bring joy to God was bigger (although just barely) than my fear. I finally had the courage to tell my pastor what I was planning to do, and he gave me permission to use the church on Monday evenings. And so, Monday night prayer began.

At first, Monday evenings consisted of me playing instrumental songs on the piano. It was simply a time when people could come and pray quietly.

As time went on, God began giving me songs. I never knew when they would come. Sometimes it would be during my personal prayer times, but other times it would just be a random time during the day. Whenever a song started coming, I would frantically grab whatever scrap of paper was near me and write as fast as I could. The words usually came faster than I could write them down.

It was at this point that God asked me to start singing some of these songs during the Monday night prayer meetings. Once again, I was faced with something that God gave me the desire to do, but I struggled to step out and obey.

I decided to begin by singing alone and recording it so I could hear myself. After listening to the first recording, I questioned whether this was a good idea. I did not think my singing sounded awful, but it certainly was not very good. I practiced for a while and finally got to the point where I thought my singing was adequate. Not that it was anything to write home about, but it was good enough to begin.

I can remember the first time I sang during a Monday prayer time. I was sitting at the piano playing the song that I planned to sing. I kept nervously playing the song over and over until I finally worked up the nerve to open my mouth and quietly sing along. I am sure my voice was shaky and far from confident, but my singing had begun. Over time, my voice developed with continued practice and kind critique from friends.

Monday night prayer had some lighter moments as well. One time I was playing the piano and singing when suddenly a cockroach ran across my sheet music. I kept playing as the cockroach walked slowly around my sheets of music. I am not too squeamish around cockroaches, so initially it was not a big deal. The next thing I knew, the cockroach was running down the keyboard. I thought, *Great, now I can flick him off.* But he stayed just out of my finger's reach.

Living

Then my heart rate started to rise as the cockroach made its way up my microphone stand and headed toward my microphone, which was sitting only an inch from my open mouth.

Anxiously, I tracked the cockroach's progress out of the corner of my eye as I tried to keep my mind on what I was playing and singing. Ever so slowly, the cockroach approached my microphone. It hesitantly twitched its antennas as it decided whether or not to make the final approach to the summit.

Finally, it made its decision and scurried its way to the top of the microphone. There it sat, twitching its antennas just an inch from my mouth. My moving lips did not seem to scare it, and I was trying to decide what to do. Should I break the prayerful atmosphere by loudly smacking my microphone? Or did I risk a cockroach jumping into my singing mouth? I was sure this would lead to an even greater interruption.

Deciding to risk it, I continued singing. My eyes were glued to my microphone as I watched for any sign that my new companion might be thinking about taking the leap.

After a few tense minutes, the cockroach turned quickly and scurried down the microphone stand and back onto my keyboard. This time he ventured a little too near my right hand, and I was able to brush him off to the floor. With that, I continued on with a wary eye for the remainder of the evening.

Overall, God used Monday night prayer in a couple of ways. He used it to minister to other people, but he also used it to impact my life. Not only did it help break me out of my comfort zone, but God also used these times to deepen my relationship with him. Most weeks I spent

The Man Behind the Mask

several hours preparing for the following Monday evening. A portion of these practice times would be spent practicing the music I planned to play, but many times they turned into personal worship times. I found myself entering into deeper worship than I had experienced before. And many times, I found myself breaking into spontaneous songs of worship to God. Over time, I began to yearn for God more than ever before.

I learned many other things through Monday night prayer, but all in all, this was where the rubber met the road. God had asked me to do something that was way out of my comfort zone, and I chose to follow him. What a joy and peace it brought to simply obey him.

The last year had been wonderful. Ever since I experienced God's unconditional love in college, I found myself in love with God. I experienced many extended times in his presence, and just the thought of God filled me with pleasure. I found myself in the bliss of simply knowing God.

Then, in April 2008, God shared some of his pain with me. While I continued to experience the bliss of knowing God, I also developed brokenness for my society. This brokenness started with an event called the "Mercy Seat." This event was a call for God's people to go to the state's Supreme Court buildings on a particular Saturday to silently and peacefully pray for the ending of abortion.

I found out about this event through some other people in my church and decided to participate. Some friends and I went to the Kansas Supreme Court building

Living

that Saturday. As we arrived, we saw a small group of people there. We joined the group and listened to a young man who was leading the Kansas group.

The young man gave some appalling statistics about abortion and then told a testimony from his own life. We spent the next few minutes praying together. After the group prayer time, we split up to pray individually for the remainder of the day.

As I prayed, I thought about some of the things I had learned recently as well as what this young man had told us. It was stunning to realize that in the United States, 1 baby was aborted for every 4 babies that were born. I was shocked that about 50 million babies had been aborted in the United States during the last forty years. The math left me stunned as I realized that every day almost 3,000 babies would perish from an abortion in the United States alone. The various statistics brought home the magnitude of the problem.

I spent the first part of the morning walking slowly around the Supreme Court building while I prayed silently. Later in the morning, I looked over the city as I walked along the back of the building. My eyes fell on an empty playground about a block away. Immediately God spoke to me. His words thundered inside me as he said, "Where are the children?" Somewhat confused, I responded that I did not know. It did seem a little strange that there were no children playing on such a beautiful spring day, but I did not know where they were. My heart broke as God continued, "These children were never born; they were never given a chance!" I did not know how to respond as I stood there stunned and filled with sorrow.

After a few minutes, I continued to walk around the

The Man Behind the Mask

building as I thought about what God had just told me. Reaching the side of the courthouse, I saw a farmer's market across the street. Suddenly, I was repulsed. Here people were buying, selling, and going about their daily routines during yet another day that nearly 3,000 babies would never see the light of day because of abortions. At that moment, God brought Deuteronomy 30:19 to my mind. This verse states that God has set life and death before us. In the same verse, God pleads with his people to choose life. I knew as a nation we were choosing death. Something had to change.

As I headed home that afternoon, I realized I had been marked. Though I still had times of joy, I could not shake the seriousness of what was going on. I was not angry at anyone, but I was disturbed by what I had learned.

- -

In August of 2008, God reminded me again about the issue of abortion. This time it was through TheCall. TheCall consisted of prayer gatherings for the purpose of repentance and asking God for his mercy and a spiritual awakening in the United States. This particular TheCall was held in Washington DC.

I did not travel to Washington DC, but the event was being broadcast live at the International House of Prayer. So I decided to go there to participate. That morning I headed over to IHOP and arrived about forty-five minutes early. I had expectations of it being good, but I had no idea what I was about to walk into. I was expecting a time of prayer and worship, but nothing like what happened.

Finding a parking spot, I walked to the front doors of

Living

the large, tin building where the broadcast was being held. I could hear music playing as I opened the door. With joy in my heart, I opened the second set of doors, which opened to the main seating area. And . . .

The instant I stepped through the door, I walked right into the tangible presence of God. I had felt the presence of God many times before but never with this intensity. The atmosphere actually felt different. It was like walking from air into water. I felt the tremendous weightiness of God's presence. I loved the feeling, but at the same time, it was awe inspiring.

I stood there for a few seconds as I tried to take it all in. The live broadcast had not started yet, but there was a live band playing worship music. I was aware of everything going on around me, but God's presence was stealing my attention.

Walking slowly across the back, I found a seat. But it did not feel appropriate to sit down. I knelt on the floor and began to worship God. Then it hit me.

Out of nowhere, I was suddenly struck with a tremendous sorrow and began to weep. Actually, wail would be a better description. I was not typically very emotional, and even if I had felt like crying, I never would have done it in public. But this hit me before I knew it was coming. Without even knowing what I was sorrowful about, I began wailing. I was not conscious of anyone around me as I wept and wailed loudly. Tears rolled down my face until it hurt to cry.

After about thirty minutes, the sorrow lifted somewhat. While I was still crying a little, I became conscious of the room around me. Suddenly I was embarrassed and wondered what the people around me were thinking. But from my place on the floor, I could hear other people weeping and wailing. Not everyone was, but it was evident God was touching many others besides me.

The sorrow lifted just long enough for me to hear what was going on around me and to get a drink from my water bottle. I could hear the broadcast begin; and I heard a speaker saying something about crying out for mercy and repentance for the issue of abortion. At this point, I realized what the sorrow was about. It was for my nation; it was for the babies being slaughtered and the parents being wounded. We were literally feeling the pains of Heaven.

With this understanding, a wave of sorrow washed over me again. I once again found myself involuntarily wailing. For another hour or so, I cried and wept until I was utterly exhausted and could not cry anymore. In brokenness, I cried out to God for mercy for my nation. I begged him to grant our nation repentance.

Finally, the intensity let up and I was able to climb into my chair. I stayed for most of the day but could not really enter into the remaining worship times because I was so exhausted by that first hour.

As I left that evening, I realized once again I had been marked. God would not let this issue of abortion alone. He had shared his sorrow with me, and I would never be the same.

Chapter 7
Dying

In 2009, God asked me to do something that made all my previous experiences pale in comparison. It shook me through and through.

I had been employed for about two and a half years at a well-paying engineering job when God told me it was almost time to quit my job. He said I should do this so I could spend more time in prayer and service to others.

God had already told me when I first started my job that it was just temporary. So I had known for quite a while this was coming. I did not expect it so soon, though.

The Man Behind the Mask

Shocked and scared, I wrote the following entry in my journal:

April 4, 2009 – God, here am I . . . I want to follow you. I want to go where you are going and do what you are doing, but I am scared. I don't want to just run off and do what I think I want to do or what I think you would want me to do. I want to be going exactly where you want me to be going. I want to follow you step by step each and every day. I seem to be leaning toward a change. An incredible, crazy, insane change . . . At least in the world's eyes it seems crazy. I just don't care anymore, God . . . I don't care about getting rich or living a "secure" and comfortable life. I just want to be going where you are going. I'd rather make a tenth of what I make now and be side by side with you then to make ten times what I make now and be wandering lost in my own ambitions. Thank you for leading me this far and giving me the willingness to follow. Here I am once again standing at a fork in the road. Both paths lead in incredibly different directions, and I am not at all sure which way you are going . . . Jesus, I need to know which way you are going. I need to be sure I am on the same path you are. You are the most important thing to me. Money, worldly pleasures, and comforts cannot even begin to compare with just being with you. So I guess I've said all this just to ask you, "Which way should I go?" Please make it clear. However you choose, but please make it clear which path I should take. You are my everything, my all in all, my reason to live. I am yours, and you are mine. I love you, God. To you be the glory, honor, and power. Forever and ever.

Dying

I continued wrestling with the thought of giving up my job. Then, around the middle of 2009, God said it was time. This hit me like a bombshell even though God had been preparing me for a while. I spent many hours praying and wrestling with this during the next few weeks. I was terrified by both the loss of income as well as the possible rejection and ridicule from my friends and family.

I had to be sure this was really God and not the "pizza I ate the night before." This was no little decision. It was a life-altering choice. It could mean the difference between a nice, comfortable life and one spent with hardship and poverty. I knew where God guides, he also provides. But was he really telling me to do this?

This brought me to the realization that I had to know for sure if what I had been hearing over the years was truly God or if it was just my own mind. It was time to get this settled once and for all. Either God was speaking and I was with him, or it was my own mind and I needed to get a grip and get on with my life.

I continued wrestling with this decision over the next few weeks. I told God I had to know for sure if it was him speaking. I asked him if now was really the time for me to give up my job. Without thinking, I opened my Bible and looked down at a random verse. The first words I saw were "Now is the accepted time" in II Corinthians 6:2. I am not one to open my Bible randomly and consider it direction from God, but this did catch my attention.

The weeks went by, and I continued praying a lot. I had to be sure this was really a God thing. Finally, I asked God not to be angry but to please give me a clearer sign. Once again, I randomly opened my Bible. I did a double take as the first words that came to my eyes were Matthew

The Man Behind the Mask

12:39 where Jesus said it is a wicked generation that seeks for a sign. At this point, I began to get it settled that this was indeed God speaking, but I was still scared out of my mind.

After many sleepless nights and miserable days, I finally mustered up enough courage to ask my sister and brother-in-law to be praying for me. I did not tell them the details, just that I really needed prayer for a possible change in my life.

After another couple of weeks, I approached my parents with what I was getting ready to do. They were shocked and warned me about the realities of what I was thinking about doing. But at the same time, they also encouraged me to follow God.

On Monday, I got ready to tell my boss that I was going to be quitting my job. I spent several hours in troubled prayer. Without thinking about it, I opened up my Bible. The first words I saw were Hebrews 3:8 (NIV) where it states, "Do not harden your heart as you did in the rebellion." Wow, I was overwhelmed. Here I was on the verge of making the decision, and God was reminding me not to harden my heart. I was now certain this really was God speaking.

I walked to my boss's office. Now was the moment. But upon reaching his office, all of my courage suddenly vanished. Every bit of strength I had just melted away. I was unable to go in. As much as I longed to obey God, my flesh was still too strong. I turned around and walked sadly back to my office.

The next day I tried again. This time I set up a meeting with my boss, and I told him I was planning to quit my job. He was shocked and could tell I was scared. He advised

Dying

me to wait a week. Then, if I still wanted to leave, he would get things in motion.

During that week, I prayed and discussed my plans with a close friend. Initially, like my parents, he also warned me of the seriousness of what I was thinking about doing and gave me some ideas of how to test it out before fully jumping in. But after a couple of days, he said he would be praying for me and that his earlier advice was not necessarily the best. As the week went by, I felt my faith wavering. I decided to put off the decision for a while.

During the meeting with my boss the next week, I told him that I was probably just going through an early mid-life crisis and I was not ready to leave my job. That evening I went home from work devastated. Here God had given me an opportunity to abandon myself to him, and I had failed miserably. I poured my misery and confusion into my journal:

May 27, 2009 – Okay, so here I am again at one of those times when it is hard to be honest, but I'm going to be anyway. So often we like to speak up when all is well, but we like to hide what is really going on when times are hard . . . Right now I am miserable. I feel rotten, sad, and totally icky . . . Oh yeah, did I mention miserable? What's the problem? Well, let me tell you. God told me to do something, and I wasn't able to do it. He told me to let something go. He told me specifically that the time to let it go was now. I came so close, so very, very close to letting it go, but at the last second (literally the last second), I chickened out and couldn't make myself do it. I know God still loves me. I am still going to Heaven, but I feel rotten that I can't seem to obey God in this. The goal of my life is

The Man Behind the Mask

to follow after and please God. To know I am disobeying God just eats me up, and to top it all off, I have been under attack from the enemy. The enemy has been stirring up some rotten feelings toward people I really love.

Okay, so the rest of this is directed to you, God. God, you know I love you. You know I yearn to give you all of me and to hold nothing back. So what the heck is going on? I hate disobeying you, and yet here I am doing it. Can't you just break the chains? Okay, I know you can break the chains . . . You've done it before many times in my life. So why not this time? I am confused. What should I do? What shouldn't I do? What the heck is going on, God? So many questions, so few answers. I love you, trust you, and long to be with you. So make a way where there seems to be no way. You parted the Red Sea. You set me free from addictions, fears, and so much more . . . Set me free. Please . . . Show me what to do . . . I am the clay. You are the potter. Get to work on me. Crush me if you have to. Break me if you have to. Whatever it takes, God!!! Teach me to walk in your ways. Rip off anything that hinders me from walking wholly after you. God, I am yours. Do with me as you please. Once again I realize how helpless I am. I am so dependent on you. Here I am. Take me. Make me. Mold me. Use me. Get honor for your name through my life. Only you can do this. Only you can do this . . . I am so weak, yet you are so strong. Forever yours, by your grace.

I spent a lot of time praying the next few months. Even though I knew God loved me, I was still miserable and would swing back and forth between knowing God is able to get me where I need to be and being overwhelmed by my own inability to obey. I was confused and broken

Dying

beyond anything I had ever experienced before. I knew I was supposed to give up my job, but I did not have the courage to do it.

As I was praying, God allowed me to feel his presence, and he told me that he still loved me. With my heart overflowing, I poured out my thoughts to God in my journal:

September 21, 2009 – Okay, God, so I'm still learning here. First of all, thank you for your relentless love. Ever since I disobeyed you a few months ago, I have been beating myself up and letting the enemy push me away from you. Jesus, thank you for letting me feel your presence again. It is totally what I live for. I am still confused about what I am supposed to be doing, but knowing you are here beside me is all I need. I know you are faithful and you will complete what you have begun in me (even though I am not even completely sure what it is you have begun). Jesus, lead on. It is my heart's desire to know you more and to follow your every move. There is nothing like being with you. You are the one that makes life worth living. Without you, I am just an empty shell going through the motions of life. Do whatever you need to do to get me where you want me to be. To you be the glory.

As the months went by, my thoughts and emotions continued to swing up and down. One day I would believe God loved me and was in control, and then the next day I would be in utter despair.

After several more months of being miserable, I was praying when God told me, "You are my beloved in whom I am well pleased. It is through your weakness that I will

The Man Behind the Mask

show my strength." This gave me peace while I continued to wait on God. I knew God would get me where I needed to be when I needed to be there. I was still disappointed in my own lack of courage to obey, but I was renewed in my reliance on the faithfulness of God. Although I was encouraged now, I would soon begin to doubt again.

- -

The year 2009 came to an end, and 2010 began. This year was going to turn out to be a year of tremendous growth.

In January, God delivered me from some anger that had been growing inside me. I had been storing up anger toward my dad for many years. The anger was subtle at first, but it had been growing faster the last few years.

My relationship with my dad was deteriorating, and I did not know what to do about it. My dad had inadvertently done some things that had hurt me, and I was slowly building a wall between us. I thought I was building this wall to protect myself, but I found out later I was actually building it out of revenge for what he had done. I was subconsciously punishing my dad with this wall of separation. It turned out this had as much of an effect on me as it did on him, if not a worse effect.

As time went on, I became more and more uncomfortable when I was around him. What started out as a little grudge began to grow into hatred. I recognized this hatred in my life, but I did not know what to do. I tried to let it go, but I could not seem to release it.

As the hatred grew inside me, I began to develop acid reflux. I did not realize at the time that the acid reflux was

Dying

related to my hatred, but that became evident later on.

It finally got to the point where I could not stand to be around my dad. When I was around him, I would try to be nice, but usually, the best I could muster was simply to not say anything at all. While I was quiet on the outside, my mind was churning with thoughts of hatred and vengeance.

I began to respond sharply to him when he said something that annoyed me. These responses came before I could stop them, and they came with a different kind of energy. It was as if something was gaining control over me. These involuntary outbursts scared me, but I did not know what to do to get free.

About this time, a teaching video was shown during a prayer meeting I attended. The video was about how to pray for others to get set free. It was not so much about what to pray as much as it was just letting God do what he wanted to do.

As I was driving home that evening, I asked God what was going on with my relationship with my dad. Very clearly the word "vengeance" came into my mind. This shocked me. I had not realized I was holding onto revenge. I thought I was just trying to protect myself from getting hurt again, but I was really harboring vengeance.

As soon as I acknowledged the vengeance in my life, the words "Vengeance is mine says the Lord" came to my mind. Somehow that set me free. I realized I was not supposed to be holding onto this vengeance. God would take care of things, and it was not mine to deal with.

At that moment, I was free. My relationship with my dad was night and day different from that point on. We did not instantly become close friends, but at least I could be around him without wanting to rip his head off. It was

The Man Behind the Mask

wonderful to be free!

It was also a surprise to discover that my acid reflux disappeared as well. The acid reflux diminished over the two days after this experience and was completely gone by the third day. To this day, I have not suffered from acid reflux again. What I could not do in my own strength and understanding, God did by speaking a simple word and phrase.

Later, in January, I found myself struggling to believe what God had told me the previous year about him loving me and using my weakness for his glory. It was at this point I had a dream or vision. It was at night, and the experience was so vivid it seemed real. It did not seem like I was asleep. I do not know if I should call it a dream or a vision, but it was far more vivid than a typical dream.

It was early in the morning, and I was still in bed when I was suddenly stricken with an immobilizing terror. I could not move or speak. Lying there frozen, I saw an inky darkness begin pouring into my room. It flowed in from above the corner of my door. I have never seen blackness that black before. My room was dark, but this blackness was darker than my room. It was utterly and completely black.

I was terrified and tried to move, but I was unable to even move a single finger. Suddenly, my body began to vibrate. It was not a shaking I could have humanly done myself; I was shaking like a cell phone vibrating. It was as if everything in me, my bones, my flesh, and every part of my body, was vibrating.

Dying

I tried desperately to tell the darkness to go away, but I could not even open my mouth. I watched helplessly as the darkness flowed down into my room and began to envelop my bed.

Suddenly I heard God say, "I am your refuge and fortress." Immediately the darkness vanished, and my room returned to normal.

As soon as the darkness had vanished, I felt my bed begin to descend. Again, I struggled to move, but I could not so much as turn my head. Fear gripped me as my bed slowly sank beneath the floor and down into darkness.

Once again, I heard God's voice as he said, "I will never leave you or forsake you." Immediately I felt my bed rise back into my room. The vibrating stopped, and the fear vanished.

Sitting up in bed, I was gripped by what had just happened. I had no idea what this experience was about. It was an incredible experience, but I did not know what to do with it. So I just wrote it down in my journal and set it aside. Later on, this experience would save my life.

Later in 2010, God checked to see if money had a hold on me. I had always given 10 percent of what I earned to the church. And every now and then I gave some extra to other charities as God asked me to. But I generally stuck with just giving ten percent. After all, is 10 percent not what the Bible says to give?

I had been out of college for two and a half years at this point. I lived very frugally and put the extra money I earned in the bank. As I watched my savings account

The Man Behind the Mask

grow, I continued to make ever increasing goals for how much to save. Once I made it to one goal, I would set a new goal. Every now and then, God would ask for a little extra for some ministry, but for the most part, I was putting my extra money into my bank account.

I was getting very close to my next goal when God surprised me with a request. He asked me to give a sizeable amount of money away to a certain ministry. I guess he was checking my heart, because he gave me an option. He said I could give either $5,000 or $10,000.

As soon as I heard this, my heart started pounding. While this was not my entire savings, it was a big chunk of it. And I had been getting excited about hitting my next savings goal. Now I had to decide if I would obey or not. If I did obey, I also had to decide which amount to give.

I really wanted to please God and give him the larger amount, but my faith was just not there. After struggling with it for a few days, I finally decided I would split the difference and give $7,500. My faith was not up for $10,000, but I did not want to give the minimum.

I nervously wrote a check for $7,500 to the ministry God had told me to give it to, but I held onto the check for few days before I had the courage to actually give it.

As soon as I had given it, I was filled with joy. And a couple weeks later, I decided to give the remainder. I wrote another check for $2,500 to make it the full $10,000. Once again, I was filled with a tremendous peace and joy.

I realized my savings account had been gaining a hold on me, and God graciously gave me the opportunity to let some of it go to remind me that it was all about him and not me.

The cool thing was after I gave it, God let me know

Dying

he had seen my obedience. At the time, they were having a performance rewards initiative at my job. If people did something outstanding, they were entered into a drawing for different rewards. There were a bunch of small prizes, but four of the prizes were thirty-two-inch flat screen TVs. Just a couple weeks after giving this money, I received a performance award. And I happened to randomly draw one of the TVs. I had never won any kind of drawing in my entire life. And now, immediately after obeying God, I got a TV. The TV was nice, but it was as if God was smiling down saying, "I really do see what you do."

Later that year, God asked me to give another chunk of money. This time it was $1,000, but once again, it was a struggle to give. I had just given $10,000, and now I was far away from the goal I had been so close to. Giving $1,000 more would set me back yet again. But I really wanted to obey. So, I hesitantly wrote the check for $1,000 and gave it away.

The amazing thing was once again God let me know he was watching. It was shortly after I gave the $1,000 away that there was a drawing at work for three iPod MP3 players. My colleagues and I were sitting in the cafeteria waiting to find out who had the winning numbers. As we waited for the numbers to be called, I sensed God smiling at me. Immediately I remembered the TV I received after giving money the last time. Now I realized I was going to get an iPod, too.

I did not even want the iPod. I already had an MP3 player. In addition, everyone at work was always asking me how I liked my TV. I did not want even more attention from winning an iPod, too.

In my mind, I kind of glared at God and told him that

The Man Behind the Mask

he better not let me win the iPod because I really did not want the extra attention. But I just knew I was going to get it.

I sat nervously as they pulled the first number out. It was not mine. Then they pulled the second number out. Again, it was not mine. I began thinking that perhaps I was just making all this up. Maybe I was not really going to win. Then they pulled the last winning number out. I did a double take. It was my number. I felt God smiling as he said, "I told you so."

As I walked up to receive the iPod, I was not sure if I should thank God or punch him in the stomach. But it helped build my faith that I was really hearing from God.

I ended up giving the iPod away to someone else because I did not need it, but this helped me get it settled that God was watching what I did. I really did not care much about the things I won, but I was so thankful to know God really saw what I did.

Later that year, I had a couple more experiences that gave me the assurance that I was really hearing God speak.

The first experience began while I was praying one day. God told me I should share my testimony at church. This made me afraid. Over the years, I had kept these experiences to myself. I was becoming convinced God was speaking, but I was reluctant to share these experiences with anyone. I did not want people to think I was crazy.

I went ahead and made an outline for what I would tell the church, but I just put it in my desk drawer. I really did not want to share it. Somewhat flippantly, I told God if he

Dying

really wanted me to share my testimony at church then he should have my pastor tell me that he was going to have people share their testimonies.

Well, less than a week later, Pastor announced that God had told him to have people share their testimonies on Wednesday nights. There was no getting around the timing and exactness of that announcement. So, I told Pastor I would share my testimony.

The second experience was in April of 2010. One of my friends really needed a job. He had sent in applications to a lot of places, but nothing had come up. He was getting nervous and wasn't sure what to do.

I spent some time asking God what my friend should do. As I was praying, God said, "The answer is on the way."

I recognized this as God speaking just like he had spoken to me many times before, but I was nervous about telling my friend. I had never actually told someone that God had shared something specific like that for them.

This was really a turning point in my life. I realized if God had spoken this, it would come to pass. But if this was just my own thoughts, then it was never really God speaking anyway.

I went out on a limb and told my friend that the answer was on the way. He actually believed me and was all excited. I was afraid because he needed a job in two weeks, and it looked impossible. If God did not come through, our faith would be shaken.

Later that week, my friend got a call from the last place he had put in an application. They wanted him to come in for an interview! We were both excited. God was moving.

The Man Behind the Mask

He went in for an interview and came back saying he had the job! We were praising God until he got another call saying they actually needed him to come in for a second interview before they gave him the job. Once again, I was a little nervous.

He went back for a second interview, and they gave him the job. Not only did he get the job, but the start date was the exact day he needed to have another job! I was amazed. How good God was. Not only had he provided, but he also had the timing just right as if to say, "See, I told you."

- -

The Fourth of July had almost arrived, and my family and I prepared to set out on the road. It was time again for our annual family vacation to Rough River State Park in Kentucky. This vacation was to turn out to be anything but enjoyable.

A few days before the trip, I noticed three tiny red spots in my armpit. Thinking they were just bug bites, I ignored them. Over the course of a few days, the spots grew a little larger, but not enough to be concerned about. But, when I woke up on the morning we planned to leave, one of the spots was noticeably larger and had started to hurt a little. I did not want to hold up the vacation, so I climbed into the van with the rest of my family, and we headed off on the ten-hour road trip.

After about five hours of traveling, the spots under my arm became very painful, and the pain was running down my arm. I was never one to take any kind of pain medicine, but my sister convinced me to take some ibuprofen. The

Dying

medicine significantly dulled the pain for the remainder of the drive.

Arriving at Rough River State Park, I proceeded to take it easy. I went out on the boat a few times and sat on the beach for a little while, but I mostly just sat around the cabin. The swelling under my arm continued for the next couple of days.

Eventually, one of the spots had grown to almost the size of a chicken egg. I was taking the maximum dose of ibuprofen, but the pain was still intense.

At this point, I decided I could not wait until we returned to Kansas to see my doctor. It was still a few days until we returned home, and the pain and swelling were only getting worse.

My mom drove me to a hospital emergency room in a small town about thirty minutes from the park. The doctor had to slice open the swollen wound. This was extremely painful since they had to stick a needle through the swollen area in order to deaden it. And even after that, the entire area was not completely deadened. The doctor then opened the wound and drained it. He had to squeeze and press the infection out. This caused considerable pain.

After all this, he packed the wound full of gauze. I was immediately put on a standard antibiotic, and a culture of my wound was sent out to a lab for analysis.

After this ordeal, my mom drove me back to Rough River State Park for the couple of remaining days of our vacation. The doctor had given me a stronger pain medicine, which helped a lot with the pain, but my wounds continued to swell.

Finally, it was time to go home. As we left Rough River State Park, we stopped by the emergency room again. The culture of my wound had come back, and it turned out the standard antibiotic was not the correct one, which is why my wounds continued to swell. So once again, my wounds had to be cut open, drained, and packed. This time I was given the correct antibiotics but was given a different pain medicine. On the drive back home, I had a reaction to the medicine. This made me feel horrible, and I was sick to my stomach the entire trip home.

Once we arrived home, I went to my family doctor. He cleaned the wounds again and sent me home with instructions to clean and bandage the wounds every day until they healed from the inside out. Daily, for several weeks, my mom graciously poured hydrogen peroxide into my wounds and applied fresh bandages.

After about a month and a half, my wounds were healed. But all the antibiotics had taken their toll on my immune system. With my weakened immune system, I came down with other illnesses over the next few months. I developed sinus infections several times. And at one point, I had a sinus infection and bronchitis at the same time. I had always been very healthy in the past, so constantly being sick was a new experience for me.

As the months continued to go by, I began doubting God again. All the sickness was wearing me down physically. And I had not been hearing God speak or feeling his presence. I was confused and began wondering if my disobedience had been too much. Maybe God had finally given up on me. Once again, I poured out my heart in my journal:

Dying

September 9, 2010 – God, I don't know what to say or do . . . My mind is too full, so I am going to pour out my thoughts on paper. I'm not saying I am right; I'm just saying this is what is pouring through my mind. I feel like a failure. I have finally come to the point that I know beyond a doubt you are real and you speak. I know you are the only thing worth living for. The problem is I can't seem to follow. You brought me to a cliff, you've told me to jump, and yet it seems you have not given me the courage to jump.

I know you are good and you know what is best, but at the moment, I am having trouble trusting you. Please help me. My hopes have been somewhat dashed since I heard you say come and yet I am unable to get out of the boat to follow.

What must I do? Is there something I need to do to break free? Please tell me. Show me what it is. If it is not really your timing, then please make it clear.

I long to follow you more than anything. Everything within me cries out for you. I know my love is weak, but your love is enough for both of us. It's just that I'm confused. Please give me direction. Please show me the way. I long to break free from the status quo, mundane religious motions. I long to truly love others as you love them and to truly follow after you.

I say that I trust you, but I'm not sure I really do. Are you really strong enough to conquer my pride and stubbornness? I know you are, and yet I wonder if I really do know. Please help me. Yours truly (only because of your love), D.T.

As the months went by, I continued to be consumed

The Man Behind the Mask

with my failure to obey God about giving up my job. Here 2010 was flying by, and I was still working at a job that God had told me to leave.

Even though God had told me it was okay and he would use my weakness, I was still broken. I was still not convinced God was strong enough to overcome my weakness.

Not a day went by that I did not wake up thinking about my failure. Once again, it became more than I could bear. On the morning of October 24, 2010, I cried out to God and said I longed to believe him, but I just could not seem to. I told him I would love him no matter what, but I really wanted confirmation that I was in his plan and that he would get me where he wanted me to be.

That morning I went to church, and my pastor happened to have the elders come up to pray for anyone that wanted prayer. I went forward to receive prayer without even thinking about what I had asked God that morning.

As they prayed for me, one lady said God had told her to tell me the word "pending." She went on to say, "My calling was there and stored up. Whatever is needed will be released when it is time. Just keep being a friend of God."

Wow, I was overcome! God had confirmed what he had spoken to me. Everything was going to be okay. He would get me where I needed to be when I needed to be there.

After over a year of struggling, I could finally say it was "well with my soul." How wonderful it was to be free of this weight that had been hanging on to me for so long.

I was amazed that all this time God was not disappointed in me and he had everything under control. I

Dying

had known this in my head, but this reality finally made it to my heart. What a peace it brought to finally have this settled in me.

Even after hearing the confirming "pending" word, I still had some health issues. During the past year and a half, I had been developing some digestion problems. It got to the point where I would get sick to my stomach unless I ate just the right amount of food. Unfortunately, "just the right amount" was not enough to meet my body's needs.

Due to the digestion problems, I had been losing weight. My normal weight had been about 135 pounds, but at this point, I had lost over 20 pounds. I was always hungry, but I could not eat enough.

Along with the hunger pains, I was also physically exhausted. I began sleeping nine or ten hours a night during the week and eleven or twelve hours a night on weekends. Even after sleeping these long hours, I was still exhausted. I struggled to stay awake and focus on my tasks at work.

During this time, I continued to have a "prayer time" each morning. But I was not hearing God or feeling his presence at all. Eventually my prayer time each morning amounted to nothing more than rolling out of bed, lying on the floor for a few minutes, and asking God to help me somehow make it through the day.

Over time, all the physical, mental, emotional, and spiritual struggles slowly piled up. I have an ability to endure hardship, but everything was taking its toll on me. Finally, around the beginning of 2011, I hit the bottom. I

The Man Behind the Mask

woke up that morning and had nothing left to give.

I slowly rolled out of bed and lay on the floor as I had been doing for a while. But this time, I could not even get up. Lying there on the floor, I realized I was literally dying. I had no physical strength left, and I was so emotionally and spiritually drained that I had nothing left to pick myself up with.

As I lay on the floor, I cried out to God and told him how sorry I was to have failed him. Then I lay there in the silence with no strength to get up. After a year and a half of fighting, I could fight no more. I resigned myself to death.

Lying there, I felt an evil oppression and honestly thought I was going to die. Then, suddenly, I remembered the dream I had a year earlier. It was as if I was living it out. Here I was with evil all around me and the grave calling my name. Just as suddenly, the words God had spoken to me in the dream pierced through me. "I am your refuge and fortress" and "I will never leave you or forsake you" reverberated throughout my being.

Life filled me as I heard these words. Immediately, strength flowed into my body, and I slowly stood to my feet and began to praise God. I realized God had never forsaken me. Praising God, I made it through the day.

From that point on, my health slowly improved and I began feeling God's presence more. It had taken me a long time, but I finally realized I could not obey God in my own strength.

Chapter 8
Learning of Him

Just a few months after coming to the end of myself, I was once again thinking about my failure to give up my job. I was not overwhelmed like I had been before, but I was confused as to what I should be doing.

I went downstairs to my work area and started crying out to God. As I was pacing back and forth, I started looking at some of the junk I had around my work area. For some time, I had wanted to throw away some stuff to make room for new stuff, but I just could not seem to bring myself to throw anything away.

Every time I started to get rid of something, I stopped because I was afraid I might need it someday. I suppose I could have thrown it out if I had to trade my life for it, but at that moment, I just could not do it.

As I was praying, I began to feel God's presence. Suddenly a power came upon me. It was something more than me.

I looked at my junk again and began to throw things away. Before I knew it, I had an entire trash bag bulging full. It was full of things that even an hour ago I would not

The Man Behind the Mask

have been able to part with.

As I looked at the trash bag, God spoke to me. He said, "Don't you know I can set you free at a moment's notice? Don't you know I have more power than you can comprehend?"

It was almost overwhelming as he went on to tell me how much he loved me. His words were very direct and firm, yet full of compassion at the same time. As he spoke, it felt like when a parent firmly but lovingly takes a child's face in their hand and tells them to look them in the eye. God reassured me that he would set me free to follow him at just the right time.

While throwing away some junk seemed like such an insignificant thing, it was the "how" that was the message. God took something I was unable to do in my own strength and suddenly gave me the ability to do it.

This experience helped settle it in me that God had things under control. I still did not know how God was going to get me where I was supposed to be, but I was confident in his ability. I finally had peace.

- -

It was August 2011, and I once again experienced God giving me a "word" for someone. Only, this time, it meant standing up and sharing it before the church.

It was Sunday morning, and I was sitting in church. I was completely unaware that God was about to speak through me. The worship time had finished, and Pastor had begun preaching. All of a sudden, I felt God's presence really strong. As I sat there experiencing his presence, I began to feel sad and broken. Then God gave me a

Learning of Him

message that I knew I was supposed to share with the congregation.

Immediately, fear gripped me. My heart started racing. I knew I was supposed to share the message, but I was afraid of getting up and sharing it. I was also a little concerned due to the fact that part of the message was to say "bleepity bleep" to indicate curse words. I was glad I did not have to say the actual curse words, but I did not feel it was appropriate to even say "bleepity bleep" in church. Especially as a "word from God." But I knew this was from God, so I decided to obey.

I waited for an appropriate time in the service and then asked Pastor if I could share something. He said I could, so I stood up and proceeded to tell the congregation that there was someone there who had been hurt by the church.

As I began to speak, it was actually hard to hold back the tears because of the brokenness I was feeling. I said I did not know if it was our church or another church that had hurt them, but some church had. I proceeded to tell whoever it was that I was a Christian, but I still made mistakes. Then I apologized on behalf of the church for sometimes being a "bleepity bleep" example of who Jesus is. I went on to tell the person that they had been letting this wound stand between them and God. I told them I was thankful for the church, but sometimes we make mistakes and do stupid stuff. I reminded them that Jesus loved them and that he would answer if they called out to him.

As soon as I finished saying everything God told me to say, peace came over me and the sorrow left. Sitting down, I was amazed at what had just happened.

The next week at church, I found out there had been a

The Man Behind the Mask

visitor the past Sunday. After the service, she had shared her story with Pastor. She told him that she had not been in church for fifteen years because she had been hurt by something another church had done to her.

Wow, I was so excited to hear this story! It was incredible and humbling to think how God allowed me to speak his words to someone else. I was so thankful God gave me the boldness to stand up and share.

- -

I had been writing for a couple of years about some of my experiences of learning to hear and recognize God's voice. I was still struggling with my failure to give up my job, and I was writing these stories to help build my own faith. But as the writing continued, it began to take on the form of a book.

I realized God had more in mind than just me. When I realized God wanted me to compile these writings into a book for others, I became scared. Here I was just coming to grips with the fact that I was indeed hearing God, and now God wanted me to share my personal stories with others. This frightened me.

I really wanted to help others, but I did not like the idea of making myself vulnerable. I knew some people would think I was crazy and other people would put me on a pedestal as if I was special, neither of which I wanted.

After working on and off for a couple of years, I finally got everything in the book that I thought should be in it. The book was still a little rough, but it was more or less complete.

At this point, God told me to show the book to a lady

Learning of Him

at my church. I really did not want to show my writings to anyone, but I went ahead and printed out the draft of my book. Holding onto the draft for a couple of weeks, I finally worked up the courage to give it to her. I told her that I felt like I was supposed to show it to her and asked her to give it back to me once she had finished reading it.

Well, as always, God knows what he is doing. Unbeknownst to me, she had just finished taking a required English class for her job. After reading through my draft, she told me she would like to help out by proofreading it for me.

The thought of her proofreading it left me both excited and scared. I was thankful for the help, but at the same time, I realized things were coming together such that I was actually going to have a book. The thought of people reading about my experiences still frightened me.

She and I went back and forth over changes and corrections for several months. Finally, the book was at the point where I thought it was good enough. I still found things that could be enhanced every time I looked at it. But God was telling me I needed to get it printed right away.

So, in August of 2011, I self-published the book through an online publishing service and ordered fifty copies to give away at my church. When the books arrived, I was really scared. It was fulfilling to actually see the results of all the effort that had gone into it, but at the same time, I desperately did not want anyone to know many of my personal stories. I really wanted to help others, but there was a personal cost.

I had already shared a copy with my pastor, and he said it was okay to hand out at church. There it was the week before I planned to give out the books, and I was suddenly hit with a paralyzing fear. It was the same fear I had experienced when I had planned to leave my job a couple of years earlier.

The fear gripped me, and I began to seriously consider not giving out the books. Then another fear began to overtake my initial fear. I began to think about all the pain I had gone through after not giving up my job. I did not want to go through anything like that again. This fear of disobeying God actually became greater than my fear of giving out the books.

While I do not consider fear to be the ideal motivator for obedience, I was thankful for this fear. I really did want to obey God. And this fear helped me step out and obey.

I gave out the books the next Sunday. It immediately brought such joy to obey God. I was actually surprised at how well most people received the book. In fact, a lot of people began to open up and tell me about their own experiences of hearing God. And later on, others shared how the book was helpful in their lives.

During the same time that I was completing the book, I was introduced to meditating on the Bible. In the past, I had read the Bible cover to cover and even studied and memorized portions of it. But I had never really seriously dug into Bible passages on a consistent basis.

To be honest, I had learned to hear from God, and I was hesitant to simply read the Bible and believe what someone else had written about God. The Bible seemed to match the God that I was getting to know, but I was not going to simply believe the Bible was without error

Learning of Him

because someone had told me it was. I knew I could rely on what God told me, but I was not so sure I could be confident in what others said, even in the Bible.

So anyway, a couple from my church started a meeting every Sunday afternoon for the purpose of meditating on God's word. The idea was to take a scripture passage, memorize it, find other related scripture passages, and ask God for revelation on the meaning of the passage. As we began, I quickly realized there were many individual verses I had heard taught completely out of context. It was amazing to see how a single verse can be used to make a point that is completely unrelated to what the verse is really about.

For the first few Sunday afternoons, we went over some various verses about meditating. Then the leaders asked for suggestions about what passage we should do next. That week, I asked God what passage we should do. He replied, "Matthew chapters five, six, and seven." I sat there stunned! This was not at all what I was expecting or wanting to hear. I had always had a difficult time memorizing, and the thought of memorizing three chapters was completely out of the realm of what I thought possible. I was thinking, "God, you can't be serious!" I mean, this was a total of 111 verses. There was no way I could memorize all those. But I was convinced this was what I was supposed to do. So I told God that I would do it, but I figured it would probably take me a few years to memorize it all.

The next Sunday, I told the group that I thought we should memorize the Sermon on the Mount. Thinking I was referring to the Beatitudes (the first few verses of Matthew chapter five), they agreed that would be a good

The Man Behind the Mask

passage. But after I clarified that I meant the entire three chapters of Matthew, they were not quite so sure.

As a group, we started working on the fifth chapter of Matthew. I found I was able to memorize much faster than I had expected. It was still a lot of work, but I discovered that memorizing the passages was not nearly as bad as I had thought it would be.

I began memorizing the verses during my commute to work, over lunch hour, and during my exercise times. I also thought about the verses at various times throughout the day.

It was during this time that I discovered God was using these verses to change me. One example is related to Matthew 5:22 and 5:44. These passages are about the dangers of anger and how we are to love our enemies and bless those that curse us. As I already related, I had struggled with anger a couple of times before. God set me free each time, but now he was going to teach me how to keep the anger from getting ahold of me in the first place.

Working on these passages during my drive to work provided my first opportunity for change. Inevitably, some jerk would cut right in front of me or perform some other crazy maneuver.

As always, a surge of anger would rise up inside of me and I would think about what an idiot they were. This had happened for years. I never really thought anything about it. I mean, doesn't everyone get mad when some idiot cuts right in front of them? But I found myself being convicted now that I was meditating on these verses.

The first time someone cut in front of me, I did not notice the anger until I had already called the guy an idiot. But as I continued rehearsing these verses over the weeks,

Learning of Him

I began to catch myself sooner and sooner.

After about a month, the verse would come to mind the moment the anger started. I would repent and actually say out loud, "I bless you," when someone cut in front of me or did something stupid. Soon I found myself not even getting angry anymore. I would simply bless the person and continue on my way. In this, I discovered freedom. All this time, the anger had been stealing from me. By learning to bless my enemy, I was free.

During these months of meditating on the three chapters of Matthew, I had another opportunity to put them into action. There was a coworker who always had something bad to say about what I did. Everyone else at work thought I did a great job and was constantly praising my work, but not this guy. He could always find something wrong with anything I did. This always made me a little upset. I never let it show, but I really did not like this guy. So once again, I put into practice the idea of loving my enemy and blessing this guy that was cursing me.

I decided I would say, "I bless you," under my breath every time I saw him. The next time I saw him, I started to quietly say, "I bless you." But I suddenly realized that I did not want to say these words. Everything in me was screaming out to curse the guy, not bless him. After all, he did not deserve to be blessed after treating me like he had.

But I obeyed God and began to bless him. It was really hard at first, but over time, it became easier and easier. After a while, I actually began to enjoy doing it. I realized once again that my anger had disappeared, and I felt free. I had no idea blessing my enemies could be so freeing for me.

Over time, this coworker even started to not be so

hard on me. But the real miracle was the transformation that had taken place in me.

Before I knew it, about three months had passed, and I had the entire three chapters of Matthew memorized. I was amazed! It had taken a lot of time and effort, but it happened a lot quicker than I expected. And the results were so worth it.

In early December, 2011, I attended a teaching that would drastically deepen my relationship with God. The teacher was from a ministry called Harvest Home. My dad had become involved with this ministry, and I had seen him grow closer to God.

Even though I had seen some positive changes in my dad's life, I was still a little cautious and skeptical. The basic concept that Harvest Home taught was the idea of encountering God through hearing, seeing, or perceiving things in our imagination. Supposedly they were not things the person thought up themselves, but were things that God put in their imagination to speak to them. Even though I had heard God speak, some of the experiences my dad talked about seemed a little strange. They did not seem bad or even unbiblical, just odd. The last thing I wanted was to get caught up in some mystical cult.

I decided to attend this teaching in December so I could find out a little more about this encountering God thing. The teaching was going to be led by a lady named Rhonda Calhoun. She and her husband were the founders of the Harvest Home ministry.

Arriving Friday afternoon, I went for the first teaching

Learning of Him

session. As Rhonda began speaking, I immediately felt the presence of God and could sense she really did know God. The teaching was good, and I did not see anything unbiblical about it. It was simply about how to come into God's presence and communicate with him.

I came back for the continued teaching on Saturday and was impressed with what was being taught. During a break in the Saturday afternoon session, I told Rhonda I knew what she was saying was true because I had experienced these things to a small degree at various times in my life. I went on to ask her how I could I make these encounters an everyday experience. In response, she asked me if I would be willing to do an "encounter" session in front of everyone so we could all learn. I hesitantly replied, "Yes."

During this session, we basically just had a time of prayer, but Rhonda helped me interact with God. In the past, I had heard God speak or had him show me something, but I had never thought to continue a dialogue with him.

We started the session by waiting quietly on God. After a little while, Rhonda asked me if I felt anything. I replied that I did not. Then she invited me to imagine that I was in a safe place, so I imagined that I was in my bedroom.

Rhonda waited a little while and then asked if I felt anything. I replied that I felt a little of God's presence. At this, she said, "Good, then we can start." Rhonda asked me if I wanted to tell God anything. I replied by telling God that I loved him. After waiting a couple of minutes, Rhonda asked me where Jesus was.

I looked around in my imagination but did not see

The Man Behind the Mask

him, so I said, "I don't know."

Rhonda asked, "So do you want to ask him where he is?"

I replied, "God, where are you?" Immediately the thought "everywhere" came to mind. "Everywhere" seemed too simplistic, but at the same time, I was filled with delight, and the word pierced through my heart in an even deeper way than when God had spoken to me in the past. The feeling reminded me of Luke 24:32 when the disciples said, "Did not our hearts burn within us while he talked with us?"

Rhonda then asked me if I wanted to tell God anything else. I said, "God, I want to know you more; I want to see your face." We waited awhile, but I did not feel or sense anything.

Then Rhonda asked me if I wanted to ask Jesus what he would like to do. So I asked God what he wanted to do. God said, "I want to know you." Immediately I was filled with intense pleasure. Rhonda asked me how it felt. I replied that it felt wonderful.

Next I asked God what his love looked like. Right away I saw a cloud. It was fuzzy and barely visible, but I could tell it was a cloud. After seeing the cloud, I waited a while, but I did not see or hear anything else.

After waiting a couple of minutes, Rhonda asked me if I wanted to ask him what the cloud meant. I asked God what the cloud meant, and he replied, "As high as the heavens are above the earth, that's how great my love is for you." These words penetrated my heart, and tears rolled down my cheeks. Then my view shifted. I saw the entire sky and a beautiful sunrise. I waited a little while, but I did not see or sense anything else. Again, Rhonda asked me if

Learning of Him

I wanted to ask him why he was showing me this. Sheepishly, I said, "God, what are you showing me?" God answered, "I made the sunrise and creation for your pleasure to show how much I love you." Rhonda asked me how it felt, but I could not really describe the feeling. It was overwhelming. It felt like it was too much, like I did not deserve it.

After waiting a few more minutes, Rhonda asked me again if I wanted to tell God anything. I said, "God, it is too much. You shouldn't have." Then I saw a hand with a ring on it, and I asked him what the ring meant. He said, "I chose you; you did not choose me." Rhonda asked me how that made me feel, and I replied that I didn't know. I did not know how to express it. Again, it just felt like this love was too much. I felt so undeserving.

Then God said, "But will you choose me?"

Immediately I replied, "Yes, God, I choose you! I love you. I choose you. Thank you, Jesus." It felt wonderful. As I enjoyed the feeling, Rhonda said, "Just let yourself feel that . . . being loved." I basked in God's love for a few minutes as I felt a tremendous peace.

We waited a few minutes, and then she asked me if I wanted to ask God where he was. I said, "God, where are you?" God replied, "I'm in you." Confused, I asked, "Why are you in me?" He said, "Because I like to be." This filled me with joy, and I replied that I liked being with him, too. Then I saw the sunrise again, and I knew it meant that he loved me. I said, "God, you are all that I am. Thank you for your love. I love being with you." Then I saw the clouds parting, and I saw a dark sky with a few stars. I realized this night sky went on and on as far as I could see. As I was filled with wonder, God told me that this was how

The Man Behind the Mask

endless his love was for me. I said, "Oh, God, thank you for your love. Help me to love you like that. I want to love you like that."

We waited awhile, and I did not feel or hear anything more. Rhonda asked me again if I wanted to say anything else to God. I said, "God, thank you. Thank you for your creation that you made to show your love for me. Thank you for your unending love. Thank you for choosing me. Help me to stay by your side."

Next I saw a chain around a neck with a ring hanging on it. I asked God what it meant. Immediately I understood it meant that his love was bound to me and that nothing could break that chain. This understanding filled me with peace.

After waiting a few more minutes, God's presence lifted, and I sat amazed at what I had just experienced.

From this experience, I realized that at first I was just listening and not talking. God desires a relationship, and I had to carry my part of the conversation. I also had to keep in touch with the feelings. A lot of times the feeling would disappear, and I had to go back to the feeling to help connect with God again.

Another thing to note is that every time God spoke, it pierced my heart. His words came with emotion, and many times literally brought me to tears. The intensity of the feelings and tears surprised me.

Rhonda went on to discuss how everything God told me in the encounter was true since it was scriptural. We also discussed how the pictures God used to show me things were at first seemingly random. They were not things I would have thought up myself. We also discussed how it takes more than simply imagining something to

Learning of Him

bring a grown man to tears for twenty-five minutes. It takes God.

Overall, it was a wonderful experience. From the first time God spoke in the encounter, I immediately recognized his voice from previous experiences in my life. As soon as I recognized his voice, I was convinced that what Rhonda had been teaching was true.

Following Rhonda's teaching, I had a couple more encounters with God that gave me a deep desire to know him more intimately. I began consistently spending at least one or two hours each night waiting on God for another encounter. I had a few little ones, but nothing much. I knew what I had experienced in the first two encounters was real, but I was frustrated at not being able to have another one like the first few.

As I continued waiting on God, lewd imaginations began filling my mind. These imaginations were a result of the pornography and sensual imaginations I had entertained when I was younger.

As I mentioned earlier, God had delivered me from these addictions, but I would still occasionally see some of these images or experience some of the sensual feelings. Whenever these images or feelings came, I did my best to push them down. I tried to ignore them, but they were distracting and annoying.

So as I just mentioned, these sexual images kept coming to mind while I was trying to encounter God. I kept asking God to take them away, but I could not seem to get rid of them.

The Man Behind the Mask

On Tuesday, December 20, 2011, I had the day off from work. I spent about five hours praying and reading my Bible at the International House of Prayer. I felt spiritually dry, but I've learned that many times God is working even when I do not feel anything.

Several times during the day, I asked God to take away these thoughts I had been having, but I did not have any breakthroughs. Leaving IHOP that evening, I still felt spiritually dry.

I went to bed that evening at about ten o'clock. As I was lying in bed, I closed my eyes and started thanking God for what he had been doing in my life. Then suddenly, I saw an image in my mind of tree pruning shears and realized God was showing this to me.

I asked God why he was showing me pruning shears. He reminded me of John 15:2 in the Bible. This passage is about how every branch that brings forth fruit is pruned so it can bring forth more fruit.

I understood God wanted to do some pruning in my life. I also understood the pruning might hurt a little, but the results would be worth it.

Then God showed me a marble, which I understood to represent my thoughts (e.g., "have you lost your marbles"). Next, he showed me a pair of small needle nose pliers. The pliers began to slowly open and close. Each time they closed, they crushed the marble a little more until it was completely powder. God told me it is the little things that ruin the vine. Then suddenly a pornography image from many years ago flashed into my mind.

As soon as I saw the image, my entire body cringed. My muscles tensed as I involuntarily curled into the fetal position. The disgust of what I had allowed into my mind

Learning of Him

was overwhelming. Without thinking, I began to cry out to God to crush this image. As I looked on, the image was crushed bit by bit until it was dust. Then the dust was swept aside. For a moment, I felt peace.

Then another image flashed into my mind, and the same process began all over again. My entire body was wracked with repulsion, and my muscles pulled me into the fetal position again. Like the previous image, this image was crushed and swept away.

This process went on for numerous images. Sometimes the feelings were so intense I thought I was going to vomit.

After about thirty minutes of this process, the images stopped coming and my body relaxed. God asked me what I saw now. I replied that I did not see anything, but it still felt like there was some residual dirt around. I felt much cleaner, but something still did not feel right. God asked me if I wanted to stop or keep going. I immediately replied that we should go ahead and get it done.

As soon as I said this, I was taken back to a memory. I saw myself watching the XXX rated video that I had found years earlier in our van. As the memory of what I had done was played out in my mind, I was overcome with the same intensity of disgust I had felt with the previous images. In the midst of these feelings, God asked me where he was when I was doing this. I looked around and saw him sitting in the room watching me.

At that moment, I was overwhelmed with intense sorrow. I began crying out to God and telling him how sorry I was that I put him through having to watch me do these things. This time the intensity of the feelings did not stop, and the image was not getting crushed. I actually

The Man Behind the Mask

became panicked because the intensity was becoming more than I could bear. Frantically, I asked God why the image and feelings were not going away. As soon as I asked, I knew the answer. I asked God to forgive me and then pleaded Jesus's blood over my sins. As I did this, the image melted away.

After this, several more past experiences came up, and each time, God told me how to deal with each one. Some were crushed immediately, and others I had to ask God how to deal with. There were some I had to acknowledge and let go of, others I had to ask forgiveness for, and still others I had to literally tell demons to leave. Each time, the image would be crushed and the dust swept aside.

Finally, after about thirty more minutes, the images stopped coming. I was exhausted as I lay back down in my bed. For a few minutes, I looked around in my mind for these images. In the past, I would have been able to easily pull these images up, but now it was different. I could still recall the images and events, but the images were blurry and not detailed. I also had no feelings associated with these memories anymore. I knew they had happened, and I knew they were wrong. But I was at peace, and the shame had been removed. It was an incredible feeling.

I took a few minutes to write the experience down, and then exhausted, I promptly fell asleep. The next morning, I woke up with such a clean feeling. It was wonderful.

As I look back at this, I realize that even though I had stopped doing these things many years before, I had never really resolved them. I had asked God to forgive me, but unwanted thoughts and feelings still haunted me from time to time. It was wonderful to finally have this dealt with. It

Learning of Him

was certainly an extremely intense experience, but the results were so worth it.

I noticed a significant difference the following couple of days. It actually felt like my brain was less cluttered. Also, I realized how I had been pushing aside thoughts without really processing them. In the past, the instant I had a thought of a woman being beautiful (not lust, just simply that she was beautiful), I would try to ignore it. It was like I was trying to suppress every thought I had about the woman. It did not matter if the thought was good or evil.

While this newfound freedom was wonderful, I found myself with a new quandary. The experience with God on Tuesday had flushed the junk out of my mind, but I was suddenly left with the realization that I had no clue how to properly process thoughts about women. I certainly did not want to fall back into lustful thoughts, but I needed to find out what to do with the thoughts that came. I knew it was not wrong to think a woman is beautiful as long as the thoughts stopped there, but I found myself awkwardly clueless.

That Thursday night, I spent some more time with God and told him how clueless I was about this whole thing. God replied, "Don't let the outward beauty (or lack thereof) distract you from the actual person inside." While I had known this idea before, it really hit home when God told me. It helped me understand it is fine to recognize that a woman is beautiful, but I need to immediately get past the outward appearance and focus on the person behind the body.

On Friday, I had a few opportunities to put this into practice. There were several occasions throughout the day

The Man Behind the Mask

when I encountered women and was able to take the first look, recognize they were beautiful, and then connect with the face and the actual person behind the face. I was able to do all this without any sensual feelings at all. In the past, I knew women were more than an object, but now I was able to engage the person without the sensual distractions.

On Saturday, I had a real surprise. It seems sacrilegious to say that God sent a Victoria's Secret catalog to our house. I do not know if he was involved, but the timing was incredible. As far as I know, we have never received a Victoria's Secret catalog at our house before, and I do not know why this one came. But it did. And it came the day after God helped me get things figured out. On top of this, I happened to be the one that went out to get the mail.

So I brought in the mail and sorted through it. I came to the bottom of the stack, and before I knew what it was, I was looking directly at a very revealing photo of a woman on the back of the Victoria's Secret catalog. It took a moment as my mind registered what I was looking at, and then I quickly stuffed the catalog under the stack of mail for my mom to deal with.

The incredible thing was that with that one glance, the only thought that came to my mind was that she was beautiful. The lustful feelings simply were not there. I did not let my eyes dwell on the photo since I understand the dangers of doing so. But it was enough for me to see that something had truly changed in me.

Besides the freedom from the lust, I also realized I was no longer looking at women simply as objects for pleasure. When I saw the lady on the back of the catalog, I saw a human being who could very well be trapped in the

Learning of Him

various bondages that are so often involved with the fashion industry. Instead of feasting my eyes on her, I spent time praying for her.

There was also another result from this experience with God. I began dreaming again. I had gone for over ten years with almost no dreams at all, and now I started having dreams several times a week

In the past, I occasionally had some spiritual dreams where God would show me things. These dreams did not occur very often, but I found that I usually had normal dreams for a few nights following these spiritual dreams. The normal dreams would always become sexually immoral in some way, and then they would stop altogether again. After this encounter where God pruned the memories, I started having dreams again. But this time, the immoral dreams did not come back.

I felt like a kid again. It was like God had restored my innocence. It was incredible to realize how much damage the sexual addictions had done. And it was really wonderful to finally be free.

Yielding to God

Chapter 9
Being Led by God

As I started to hear God speak more frequently, I began learning more about being led by him. More and more, I was finding occasions to follow his leading.

One particular occasion began on a Saturday morning in early 2012 as I was spending time in prayer. God prompted me to go for a drive. So I climbed in my car and headed out. I had no idea where I was going, so I just told God to lead me.

Pretty soon I was cruising down the highway while wondering where I was going to end up. I was on my way to somewhere, but I did not know where.

After driving for a few minutes, the thought occurred to me to go to a local Christian bookstore. I did not know if

The Man Behind the Mask

it was God's leading, but I went ahead and took the next exit and started in the direction of the bookstore.

Arriving at the bookstore, I browsed through the book section. I kept asking God what I was supposed to be doing, but I did not hear anything. After looking around for a while, I wandered over to the music section where I came across a good sale on some music CDs. Selecting a couple CDs, I made my purchase.

I looked at my watch and realized it was time for lunch. So I headed to a Kentucky Fried Chicken restaurant.

Just as I was getting ready to pull into a parking spot, God told me, "Go to McDonalds." I thought that was a little odd, but then again, so was driving aimlessly around town. So why not?

I drove to the nearby McDonalds and parked my car. Going in, I ordered chicken nuggets and fries, and after my order was ready, I found a long table with bar stools, close to a TV playing the sports channel.

Sitting down, I looked around and wondered why God wanted me to eat here. After a few minutes, a couple with two young boys came in. The youngest boy, who was probably about six years old, had spiky hair and was full of energy.

The family headed to the counter to order. While they waited in line, the youngest boy came over, sat on the stool in front of me, and stared at me with a huge grin on his face.

I asked him what he was up to. He responded that his family was there to have lunch. Trying to keep from smiling, I thought, *No, really?* We talked a little more and then I continued to eat. All the while, he kept looking at the TV for a few seconds and then looking back at me with

Being Led by God

that same big grin.

After a few minutes, his family came over, and I smiled at them as their son asked if they could sit with me. His parents asked me if it was okay. I replied that it was fine.

As they sat down, the parents introduced themselves and their two boys. Then they bowed their heads and prayed. The prayer was not one of those well-rehearsed "before you eat" prayers, but it was more like they were actually talking to God.

As they said "Amen," I chimed in and said, "Amen, sounds like you know Jesus." To which they responded that they did.

We talked for quite a while about our faith. The boys joined in, too, and I was able to encourage them in their walk with God.

One of the boys also brought up something about a horrible auto accident his dad and brother had been in. So his mom and dad related the story and how God had helped them through the difficult time of recovery.

Overall, it was great to meet up with someone I did not know and yet within minutes realize we were "family." Also, something else was interesting. Typically, I am somewhat self-conscious when I talk about my faith in public, but this time that was not the case at all. I found myself sharing some of my testimony with them, and all the while, I realized everyone sitting around us was listening in on our conversation.

After a great time of fellowship, we said our good-byes and headed in our separate directions. I still think of this family every now and then and pray for them.

It was incredible how God had set things up for us to

meet. I always wonder what impact there was. Maybe someday in Heaven we will meet again and learn the whole story.

In February 2012, I had an opportunity to get involved with outreach to those involved with abortions. Ever since my experiences at the Mercy Seat and TheCall, I continued to be burdened with the issue of abortion and those involved. Recently I had learned about an organization called 40 Days for Life. This organization helped organize prayer and outreach outside abortion clinics. Each spring and fall they had forty days set aside for people to peacefully pray outside abortion clinics and compassionately hand out information about help resources for alternatives to abortion.

I had spent a lot of time praying for this issue, but the idea of actually standing outside an abortion clinic seemed a bit frightening. However, my compassion for these babies and their parents compelled me to do something. So I hesitantly signed up to participate in a 40 Days for Life outside a local abortion clinic. To participate, everyone had to sign an agreement that they would obey the law and remain peaceful. It was not a protest, but a prayer and outreach gathering. It was not to point fingers, but to pray for mercy and provide help for those going to the clinic.

The first day came, and I drove hesitantly to the local clinic. I parked at a nearby business that had agreed to let us use their parking lot. I then sat for a minute as I pondered what I was about to do. As I stepped out of my car, I was a little nervous. It made it easier since there were

Being Led by God

other people there, but I was still not sure what to expect.

Joining the group who had arrived to pray, we introduced ourselves and then spent about an hour praying together. After this prayer time, most of the group left, leaving a few of us to stand our "watch." As I stood outside the clinic, my heart was torn. Abortion became much more real as I watched women go into the clinic. I realized that at that very moment, babies were being torn apart and sucked into the special vacuum in the building just a few yards in front of me.

I started to get overwhelmed as I prayed. The reality of what was going on was just too much for me. I cried out to God and asked him how anyone could allow their baby to be killed. He responded, "Blindness."

I went home that evening and felt very overwhelmed by it all. As I poured out my heart to God, he told me to read Isaiah 42. Relief and peace flooded me as I read Isaiah 42:1-7. This passage talked about God's servant bringing justice, not shouting, not being discouraged, and opening the eyes of the blind. And it went on to talk about God taking hold of his servant's hand. This passage seemed to be talking about me that day. I did not remember ever reading this passage before, but God told me to read it, and it was just what I needed.

Over the course of the forty days, I went to the clinic several times. On one occasion, I met a lady who was also there to pray. We prayed together for a while, and then she began telling me why she came so regularly to pray outside the clinic.

As a young lady, she had been raped and became pregnant. She had decided the best thing to do was to get an abortion. After the abortion, she tried to carry on with

The Man Behind the Mask

life as usual. But the abortion haunted her. She started drinking, among other things. Soon her life was in shambles. In desperation, she cried out to God for help, and he forgave and helped her.

Now she stands outside clinics to pray and reach out to others. She hopes she can spare others from the agony she went through. I have had the privilege of standing outside the abortion clinic with her. Sometimes people come and tell her that she has no business telling others what they can and cannot do. In response, she calmly and compassionately answers with her testimony.

The more time I spent outside the clinic, the more my heart ached for those who felt they had no other choice but to abort their baby. While abortion may seem like the easy answer, it is not. I pray that those seeking abortions would find out about the organizations that provide emotional, physical, monetary, and spiritual help to those in need.

Shortly after I got involved with 40 Days for Life, God once again told me something that would test my faith. Only this time, it would mean *not* doing something.

You see, the church I attended had renovated an old nursing home and was using it to provide housing for people in need. Over the years, it was amazing how God provided the finances for the ministry. From time to time, some major expense would arise, and one way or another provision would miraculously come. And now, the ministry was in need again.

The previous insurance provider for the church had decided to stop covering the ministry, so the church was

Being Led by God

looking for a new provider. There was difficulty finding another provider, but one was finally found that was willing to cover it. But before they would provide insurance, they required locks to be put on all the outside doors.

This might seem like a small thing, but the cost of providing the special safety locks and entrance keypads was up in the thousands of dollars. And the church did not have the money.

I had been saving my money since the last time God told me to give a large chunk of money, and I was at the point where I could have written a check for the entire amount needed. I prayed about whether or not I should give the money to the church, but God did not respond. As time went on, I became concerned because the church really needed insurance, but the money was not coming in. I continued praying about it, but God was not responding.

I was thinking about going ahead and writing the check. But God finally spoke. I was at work at the time and was walking around the outdoor path over my lunch hour. The weather was beautiful, and I was enjoying the outdoors as I once again posed the question to God as to whether or not I should give.

God responded by saying, "Look over there." A little surprised, I looked in the direction God indicated. All I could see was a small portion of a warehouse. The warehouse sat across the highway from where I was, and there were two trees in front of me that blocked my view of everything except an air vent on the warehouse roof.

God asked, "What do you see?" In bewilderment, I replied that I only saw the heating/cooling vent on top of the roof. God said, "Tell me about the vent."

The Man Behind the Mask

At this point, I was really confused and wondered if I was just making this whole conversation up. But I recognized it as God's voice. So I began to tell God the vent was used to take air in and out of the building. I then told him it had fans, filters, and other such things.

By now I was feeling a little goofy. I mean really, explaining a building's heating and cooling system to God. Seriously, what did this have to do with anything?

I finally got to the point of saying there was a thermostat that controlled when the vents were opened or closed. At that moment, God said, "That is it!" And then I realized what the point was. There was something that controlled when the vent opened and closed. God was the control, and I should only open the vent (give money) when he told me to.

This whole conversation seemed crazy, but I realized it was more than just my own thoughts. I had heard "look over there" at the precise moment when the vent was in my view. Only a few moments earlier or later and the trees would have hidden the vent from my view. And it was such a crazy example; I never would have come up with it on my own.

So now I knew I was not supposed to give any money unless he told me to, but he still had not given me a clear yes or no. So I decided I would wait on God even though it naturally seemed best to go ahead and give to the church.

Well, the days continued to go by, and still the church did not have the money for the locks. I became afraid the money would not come in and wondered if I should just go ahead and give. I mean, maybe I was just not able to hear God's voice for some reason. Perhaps he was unable to tell me to give now. But as I rehearsed what God had told me

Being Led by God

about only giving when he told me to, I realized I was being motivated by fear instead of by God. This realization surprised me, and I realized there were many other times in my life when I had done something out of fear instead of trusting God. So I told God I was going to trust him and wait for his leading.

After some time, the money still had not come in, and the pastor of our church had a special meeting where he invited people to come hear about the ministry and give financially if they wanted to. Not sure what to do, I hesitantly went to the meeting.

At the end of the meeting, the plate was passed for people to give an offering. I kept thinking God would tell me to give, but he did not. I sat there as the plate came closer and closer. All the while my embarrassment grew. I realized the plate was going to go past me, and I was not going to put anything in it. It was not like everyone was watching me, but it felt strange to be at the meeting and not give, when my friends on each side of me put something in the plate. Once again, I realized a wrong motivation. Here I was thinking about disobeying God by giving money, when he had told me not to give unless he said to. So I let the plate pass by me without giving anything. I remember sitting there wondering if this was really God. I mean, really, how could it not be God's will for me to help my church in a time of need? I went home that evening confused but determined to obey God.

Soon I learned that enough money had not come in, and the insurance provider said they could not help us. Now I was really confused. I kept asking God what was going on, but he did not reply. I was seriously thinking I had missed it on this one. Perhaps I had heard wrongly.

The Man Behind the Mask

While I was worried, God had everything under control. The church ended up finding another insurance company that was willing to insure the ministry. The wonderful thing was they were not going to require the locks on the doors. And, better yet, the insurance premiums were significantly less than either of the other providers. Wow, I had to once again admit God knew better than I. If I had given the money, the ministry would have been forced to put locks on the doors, and they would have been stuck with a higher insurance premium. So not giving was actually better than giving.

I was once again put in my place. God was God, and I was not. How it pays to listen.

In September of 2012, I had another experience of being led by God. This occurrence happened as I was driving to the Wednesday evening service at my church. I was about three blocks from church when I saw a young guy sitting on a stone wall beside the road. God told me to stop and talk to him. I was already past him, so I drove around the block. When I came back around, I could not find a good place to park.

Without a parking spot, and realizing I was going to be late to church, I started toward church again and decided I would just pray for the guy. God was quick to remind me that he had not told me to pray for the guy, but to stop and talk to him.

So once again I drove around the block. This time I found a place to park about half a block away. Parking my car, I got out and walked apprehensively over to the guy

Being Led by God

while trying to figure out what I was going to say.

As I approached him, I simply said, "Hey, how are you doing?" I could see tears in his eyes as he said he was not doing very well.

I sat down beside him as he covered his face with his hands and started crying. Unsure what to do, I just sat there and let him cry for a while. When his crying subsided, I told him I was not trying to pry, but I was willing to listen.

He looked me in the eyes for a few seconds and then poured out his story. He was broken as he explained he had just cheated on his girlfriend and was not proud of it. He told me he regretted it and then started crying again.

I let him cry some more, and then I asked him if he knew God. He said, "Kind of." He said he knew there was a God and that he was his "higher power." I asked if he knew Jesus. He replied, "No." So I told him the basics of the Gospel and how Jesus had changed my life. Then I started to get a little deeper into the Gospel, but God stopped me and told me I had said enough. So I just listened to the guy and let him cry again.

After a few minutes, I noticed a girl walking along the sidewalk toward us. She was wearing pajamas and holding some clothes in her arms as she eyed me apprehensively for a few seconds before approaching.

She walked up to the guy and started talking to him. After a minute, I understood she was the girl he had just been with. She began making plans to leave, and God told me it was okay for me to leave as well.

As I got up to go, the guy looked me in the eyes. He gratefully told me thank you. I put my hand on his shoulder and told him I would be praying for him. Getting into my car, I headed to church. I was a little late, but I was

The Man Behind the Mask

so glad I had stopped. What a blessing it was to simply share God's mercy with someone.

Later in the year, I experienced being led by God again. It was the middle of December and time for some Christmas shopping. As I left my house, I asked God to let me partner with him in whatever he wanted me to do. Then I asked him if there was anything he wanted to tell me. He said, "I am going to take you where you do not want to go." Well, I was a little sorry I had asked. This did not sound like much fun at all.

I quickly forgot about this conversation as I went about my shopping. I had a list of items I needed to get, and I looked at the list many times as I was at the store. But somehow I kept overlooking where I had written down "white elephant gift."

Thinking I had finished my shopping, I headed home. Driving down the road, I suddenly remembered I had not purchased a white elephant gift for my family's gift exchange. I happened to be near the Goodwill store at the time, so I decided to stop and see if I could find a gift.

As I went into the store, I noticed a man sitting with his back against the front of the store. He looked like he was probably homeless, and the thought crossed my mind that I should give him some money.

I went ahead and entered the store, but I could not get the homeless guy out of my mind. I wandered up and down the aisles for awhile but did not find anything for a white elephant gift. Still thinking about what I should do for the man outside, I walked out of the store. The man was still

Being Led by God

sitting there, so I decided to give him some money.

I pulled some money from my wallet and held it out as I approached him. He stood up and took the money. As he looked at how much I gave him, he smiled and proceeded to give me a hug.

I was not expecting a hug, and my first reaction was fear. My mind immediately went on "red alert" as I maintained awareness of where his hands were and where my wallet was. His hands did not go anywhere near my pockets, so I started to relax. I realized the hug was simply his expression of thanks.

As my body relaxed, I started to take in more of what was happening. I became aware of the man's filthy clothes and body. Then my nose caught the unpleasant smell of body odor and a faint hint of beer. My mind was immediately repulsed by all of this, yet my spirit was joyful and at peace.

After releasing me from the hug, he asked me to pray for him. Taking his hands in mine, I asked God to help him. Immediately the man said, "Make sure to tell God that I am homeless." So I told God that he was homeless and needed a place to stay. I got to the end of the prayer, and before I could say "Amen," the man said, "Make sure to say, 'in Jesus name.'" So I said, "In Jesus name, amen."

After praying for him, we started talking. As we talked, I let my eyes wander to the people passing behind him. Immediately the man jerked his head around to see what was behind him. Just seeing the people walking by, he turned back to me and asked what I had been looking at. I replied I was just looking at the people walking by. He said, "Don't do that; it makes me nervous." I realized my eye movement had been enough to make him think

The Man Behind the Mask

someone was coming up behind him to hurt him. Sadly, I began to understand the fear that homeless people live with.

After talking for a minute, I asked him if I could sit down and chat with him. He said, "Sure." So I sat down beside him on the sidewalk. He was more than happy to talk, and we chatted for a while. He was a little hard of hearing, so we had to talk loud enough that anyone passing by could hear what we were saying.

As we were talking, I became aware of the people walking in front of us on the sidewalk. Some people completely ignored us, but many people looked at us as they passed by. It was obvious from people's expressions that some were disgusted at the sight of us talking. Other people appeared to be uncomfortable seeing us. And it looked as if some felt guilty for passing by without helping.

I actually began to feel very self-conscious and even a little embarrassed. The more people that passed by looking at us in disgust, the more embarrassed I became. My mind started pleading with me to leave because it did not like the shame, but my spirit was telling me to stay. I began to realize this must be how people looked at Jesus when he was helping the prostitutes and tax collectors of his day. I suddenly felt closer to Jesus than I had in a long time. Perhaps this was a tiny taste of what it was to share in his sufferings.

The man's voice broke into my thoughts as he asked what my name was. I told him my name, and he answered with his name. I asked him how long he had been on the streets, to which he responded, "Too long." It quickly became evident he was still a little nervous and was afraid

Being Led by God

to tell me too much about himself.

He asked me what I thought about his skin. Looking at his black skin, I said, "You have skin, I have skin, God made us both." Next he asked about the church I went to. I told him our pastor had adopted African American and Chinese kids. When he heard that, he said, "You're lying to me!" I looked him straight in the eyes as I told him I was telling him the truth. Shocked, he said he wished everyone saw people like he and I did.

As I stood up to leave, he asked me to pray for him again. I had just started to pray when he said, "Ask God to keep me safe." So I asked God to keep him safe and for his angels to watch over him. The homeless man continued, "Yes, day and night, ask him to keep me safe day and night."

As I finished praying for him, he hugged me again. Then I walked away as he loudly proclaimed, "Thank you! It was nice meeting you!" I replied, "It was great meeting you, too." To which he replied, "Thank you! It was nice meeting you!" He kept saying this over and over as I walked away.

I am so glad God set up this meeting. It gave me a glimpse into the shame and loneliness that homeless people deal with. I realized that not only do these people need a meal, but they also need friendship and deliverance.

Chapter 10
Doing Life with God

In October of 2012, I found myself in a spiritually dry time. For about a month and a half, I had not been feeling God's presence during my prayer times. This made me frustrated, and I started complaining to God.

After a couple weeks of complaining, God told me I was just trying to feel his presence and was not really asking him what he wanted. This convicted me a little. So for the next week, I spent my prayer times simply praising and worshiping God even though I was not feeling his presence.

As I was praying one Sunday afternoon, God told me I had been treating him like an object. Immediately my heart was broken, and I fell to my knees as I told him I was sorry. I knew from past experiences what it meant to treat

The Man Behind the Mask

someone like an object. It meant I was treating him like a prostitute. A man who goes to a prostitute is interested only in getting pleasure from her and cares nothing for the thoughts, feelings, or desires of the lady herself. So it was with me; I was simply coming to God for the pleasure of being with him, without ever asking what he wanted to do.

I repented from treating God like an object. The next week was spent simply focusing on him and asking him what he wanted to do during my prayer times.

I was praying that Tuesday evening, when I felt God's presence in a very strong, wonderful way. But even as I was feeling his wonderful presence, I was not distracted by the feelings. My focus was on him and not simply the pleasure of being with him. The feelings merely helped me to praise him all the more.

Later that same week, I felt spiritually dry again. I was having my morning prayer time, but I was not feeling God's presence at all. I told God it was fine if this was what he wanted. But I asked if there was anything blocking me from feeling his presence. He responded, "Your mind." In response, I asked him what needed to happen. He replied that my mind needed to be renewed. I knew memorizing scripture helps to renew a person's mind, so I asked him if there were some scriptures I should memorize. But God replied that he would take care of it.

Right after he said that, I saw an image in my mind of a carpenter's plane and a wooden board. Immediately I understood the board represented me. As I looked closer at the board, I could see it looked fairly smooth, but then I noticed a bump toward one end.

I asked God what the bump was, and he said, "Pride." Next I looked toward the other end and saw another bump.

Doing Life with God

Hesitantly, I asked him what this bump was. He replied, "Selfishness." This broke my heart because these are two things I absolutely do not want in my life. I knew God was strongly opposed to these things, and they were damaging both to me and those around me.

With God's prompting, I began telling him, "You are my king," over and over for a few minutes. Slowly these words settled into me. Again with God's prompting, I began saying, "You are my husband," over and over. I was filled with joy. It was refreshing to remember he was God and I was not. Everything was all about him and what he wanted. Not about me and what I wanted. But at the same time, his desires would bring joy and fulfillment to me as well.

Around the beginning of 2013, God told me to start fasting from food regularly. I had fasted many things over the years to make more time for God, but I had always struggled when it came to food. I really wanted to obey God, so I decided to go ahead and give up one meal a week. This was to be a real test of my faith.

You see, I had not been able to fast food ever since my digestion problems occurred after not giving up my job. Every time I tried to fast, my stomach would start to hurt so much that I would eat in order to stop the pain.

But now that God had told me to fast, I decided to go for it. It was Saturday morning, and I went without breakfast. I waited a couple hours expecting the pain to begin, but nothing happened. I thought I was healed.

Then, suddenly, the pain hit. It started out as just a

The Man Behind the Mask

little stomach pain, but quickly increased. Soon my stomach was in excruciating pain, and pain began shooting down my arms. I was not sure if the cause of the pain was something physical or spiritual, but the pain was becoming unbearable. I began to feel lightheaded, and my vision blurred as I started to see stars. As the pain increased, I felt like I was going to pass out.

Then, as the pain became more than I could bear, a boldness suddenly rose up within me. I said out loud, "Satan, I do not care if this kills me, I will obey God." No sooner had those words left my mouth than the pain faded away. It was like a switch had been turned off and the pain just disappeared. I went ahead and fasted until lunch with no further problems.

Almost every week after that, I continued to give up a meal. And I never had any pain again. While my body did not like giving up a meal, it was a refreshing reminder each week that I should not live by bread alone, but by every word that God speaks. I should not do things by my own might or power, but by God's spirit.

In early 2013, I learned more about God. A friend of the family got sick and died unexpectedly. He was only forty-five when he passed away. He left a widow and young, fatherless children behind. Although I was not personally close to him, it hit me hard.

Recently God had been teaching me about Micah 6:8 where God asks his people to do justly, love mercy, and walk humbly with him. With this man's death, I was suddenly a little angry at God. Here he had been telling me

Doing Life with God

to do justly and love mercy, but I could not see how it was just or merciful for God to allow this man to die and leave a widow and fatherless children behind.

As I was struggling with why God would allow this, I decided to spend some time in prayer. I sat down and closed my eyes, but I had trouble entering God's presence because I was upset with what he had allowed.

I thought maybe some music would help, so I turned on my MP3 player and randomly selected a song to play. The song happened to be "Oh Taste and See (That the Lord is Good)" by Misty Edwards. As soon as it started, I felt anger rising up in me. Somewhat sharply, I told God, "How can you be good and still allow him to die?" I did not hear God respond, and I did not feel his presence.

As I sat there, I told God I was sorry but that I was hacked off at him and was uncomfortable trying to come into his presence. I asked him to help me because I did not want to let this build a wall between us.

Suddenly, I sensed God's presence behind me. I felt him wrap his arms around me. His love blanketed me, but at the same time, I still sensed the bitterness in me.

Again, I asked God how he could claim to love us and still allow this to happen. At that instant, I saw Jesus hanging on the cross. My anger melted away as I was reminded of his great love for me. I still did not understand why he had allowed this man to die, but I knew he loved me. So, though sorrow is natural, I could still taste and see that God was good.

The following Sunday, God asked me to share this experience at church, and thankfully, I obeyed. Several people thanked me for sharing this because they had been dealing with the same feelings.

The Man Behind the Mask

This experience reminded me to never let bitterness or anger separate me from God. He is the only one that can truly heal a heart; all that is required is to come to him.

Well, April 2013 rolled around, and along came an opportunity to learn of God's peace that passes understanding. Surprisingly, this opportunity came in the form of an impacted wisdom tooth.

When I first found out I had a wisdom tooth, my dentist said I could go ahead and get it pulled out or I could just wait and see if it caused any trouble. He said I only had one wisdom tooth and that it was on the top where there was plenty of room for it. Not wanting to get it pulled, I said I would just wait and see.

Well, the years had gone by, and every now and then my wisdom tooth hurt a little but never too bad. Then, in 2012, there were several times when it became fairly painful. Finally, in April of 2013, the real fun began.

There were several times in April when my tooth hurt a little and was putting pressure on my other teeth. But I figured it was just another round of the same thing I had experienced before.

In the third week of April, the pain became more constant. It was still not terrible, but the pain was there more than it was not. And it started messing with my sinuses such that I had a runny nose. Even with this, I expected it to pass like it had before.

On the following Monday morning, God gave me a heads-up. I was having my morning prayer time. But honestly, I was not expecting to hear anything from God because the last few weeks had been spiritually dry.

I was sitting quietly in bed when I suddenly felt God's presence. Filled with joy, I immediately thanked him and asked what he wanted to do. He replied that he wanted to take me out for ice cream. I was surprised but replied, "Okay."

The next thing I knew, God was once again taking me on an adventure in my imagination. He and I were in an ice cream store that had lots of flavors to choose from. He asked me which flavor I wanted.

I started thinking about the various flavors I could choose from, but I decided to ask him which flavor I should get. I said, "God, why don't you choose for me?" He replied, "Okay," and then told the lady at the counter that I would like one scoop of rocky road with a scoop of tin roof sundae on top.

I was confused as I held the cone with the two flavors of ice cream on it. While these were flavors I liked, they were not flavors I would have chosen at a store like this. I figured God knew my favorite kinds of ice cream, so I asked him why he had chosen these flavors for me. He replied, "There is a rough road ahead of you, but I will be a roof over your head."

With those words, God's presence lifted, and I sat in amazement as his words resonated within me. I was not too keen on the idea of a rough road ahead of me, but I was thankful God was going to be a roof over me.

During the day on Monday, my tooth really started to hurt. By the afternoon, it was messing with my sinuses to the point where I could not breathe through my nose. I already had an appointment with my dentist the next day to get my teeth cleaned. So I figured I could ask about getting

The Man Behind the Mask

my wisdom tooth removed.

On Tuesday, my tooth was still hurting but not quite as intensely as it had on Monday. I went to get my teeth cleaned that afternoon and told my dentist about the pain. My dentist does not do things unless he really thinks they are necessary. So I was actually hoping he would just say the pain would pass and there was no need for it to be removed. But that was not the case. As soon as I described my symptoms, he immediately replied, "Get it out." Then he referred me to an oral surgeon who could extract it. This was not what I wanted to hear. I had heard many horror stories over the years about wisdom tooth removals, and I was not looking forward to this.

As I made an appointment to get my tooth extracted a week from Friday, I began wondering if the whole thing with God taking me out for ice cream was about my wisdom tooth. This whole thing could be the rough road, but somehow, even with all the pain, I was surprised God would talk to me about something as insignificant as a wisdom tooth.

Over the next few days, I was filled with fear about my upcoming tooth extraction. While I kept my calm demeanor on the outside, I was really frightened on the inside. I had never even had a cavity in my life, and with all the terrible experiences I had heard from other people, I was afraid. I even started waking up at night with my heart pounding and fear running through me.

As the fear continued to grow, I thought about what God had told me when he took me out for ice cream. He had said he would be a roof over my head. Looking for further clarification, I searched the Bible for passages about God being a roof over our heads, but I did not find anything that seemed applicable. Finally, I asked God what a roof over my head meant. Immediately the word "shelter" came to my mind. So, I searched for shelter in the Bible and found lots of verses. The chapter that really ministered to me was Psalm 91, which talks about how those who dwell in the secret place of God shall abide under his shadow. Every time I began to fear, I would rehearse this passage of scripture. Rehearsing the scripture seemed to help when the fear came, but it was a constant battle to keep my mind on the verses.

In the middle of Sunday night, I woke up again with panic running through me. But this time I felt God's presence, and he gave me a song. The words just flowed out of my mouth:

Wherever I go,
You are always near.
For you are living inside me,
I've got nothing to fear.

Peace filled me as I sang this song. It was not a peace I had to work up. It was just there. For the next two days, I was filled with joy and peace. And I could not get that song out of my head.

On Tuesday, I was at work when my mind began to wander once again to my tooth extraction and the horror stories I had heard from others. Only this time, I felt God's presence, and he showed me sitting in the doctor's chair preparing for surgery. All I saw was the empty shell of my body, but inside my body was Jesus. It was incredible. I knew he was with me, and once again the joy and peace flooded my heart.

The Man Behind the Mask

I was filled with this joy and peace for the remainder of the week. Every day I expected the joy and peace to wear off, but it did not. In fact, I was getting to the point of being almost giddy with excitement. This was completely unlike me. I did not tend to get excited about much of anything, and here I was excited about a tooth extraction. Go figure. God is so amazing.

Well, Friday arrived. I woke up with peace and joy in my heart. I was not nervous at all. My mom drove me to the doctor, and I entered the surgery room. I took note as I realized the room was arranged just like God had showed me earlier in the week. Sitting down in the chair, I was at perfect peace and simply placed myself in God's hands.

The next thing I knew, I was waking up from surgery and finding out that everything went great. It was also a relief to find out I was nice to the nurses as I was coming out of sedation. Although I guess I kept asking my mom over and over what time it was and if I had any stitches, I did not say anything embarrassing. And although I do not remember it, evidently I was thanking the nurses every time they did something for me. I was so thankful to God. The surgery was over, and now it was time to go home to Advil, ice cream, and smoothies.

To be honest, this was the first time I truly experienced the peace that passes understanding. And I actually thanked God for my wisdom tooth. For years I had thanked God that I *only* had one wisdom tooth, but at the same time complained that I had one at all. Now I actually found myself wishing I had another wisdom tooth so I could go through this experience again. Who would have thought the week leading up to my wisdom tooth extraction would be one of the most enjoyable weeks of my life? Truly it is not what we go through but who we go through it with that matters.

As I just finished writing the previous section about going through life with someone, it reminded me that I am almost thirty years old and still single. At least I am single in the way that most people see it.

The other day I was driving down the road when I saw a man and woman. They were holding hands as they walked along the sidewalk. Immediately a tinge of longing pricked my heart. Something in me longed for an intimate relationship with someone.

This was not the first time I had felt that longing. The first time I felt it, I thought maybe I should consider looking for a girlfriend. But as time went on, I realized the longing only came when I had allowed my relationship with God to grow cold. As soon as I started spending quality time with God again, my longing for an intimate relationship disappeared, and the contentedness returned. This realization helped me understand that even though I was single, I was not alone. I never have to be alone because of my relationship with God.

Now I just want to make it clear. I am not saying that no one should get married. And although I do not have any plans to get married, I am not saying I will never get married. I am just saying that true fulfillment comes from simply knowing and following God. For some this means marriage, and for others, it means staying single.

When I was in my younger twenties, family and friends would ask me if I had a girlfriend yet. To which I

The Man Behind the Mask

would simply reply, "No."

As I approached my mid-twenties, they began telling me about some nice girl they had met or they would offer to pass along some girl's phone number. To which I simply replied, "No thanks."

Now that I am approaching my thirtieth birthday, people's comments have changed. People say things like, "I'm sure the perfect girl is out there. You will find her." Or with a hint of sadness in their voice, they say, "God's timing is perfect. He will bring you a wife at just the right time." At first, I was not sure how to respond to these comments. Usually I just nodded my head. To be honest, I was not looking for a wife, and I really was content being single. However, I began to realize these people were actually concerned and sad for me. With this realization, I changed my response to their comments. My response became more along the lines of, "I am single and content."

While this response is often met with a surprised or confused look, it is the truth. I do not need to get married to find fulfillment, when a relationship with God leads to true fulfillment. If God leads me to get married at some point, then I will, but if not, I will remain happily single.

Around this time, I had once again been spiritually dry for a few weeks. I did not know why I was not hearing God or feeling his presence. Then one day out of the blue, God told me to visit someone. As I visited with this man, I realized that he needed some help, but I did not know how to help him.

When I got home that evening, I sat down on my bed

and spent some time praying. I asked God for help because I did not know how to help this man. Immediately God showed me long, metal blacksmith tongs. I asked God what these meant. To which he replied, "Just watch."

I watched as the tongs were put into a fire. Then the short end of the tongs heated up and began to glow orange. After this, a hammer pounded the end of the tongs. Blow after blow, the hammer came down on the tongs. After several hammer strikes, the end of the tongs had been formed into sharp cutting edges like tree shears.

As I watched, the sharp end of the shears slowly turned toward me. I became very uncomfortable as the shears moved toward my chest. I began to cry out to God. I kept saying, "No! No! Please no!" but the shears kept getting closer. I tried to move back, but my back was pressed against the headboard of my bed. Again, I cried out, "No!" But at the same time I was telling God no, I really hoped he would continue because I trusted him to only do good.

Finally, the shears plunged into my chest and began to cut around my heart. I did not feel any physical pain as the shears slowly cut around my heart, but I was extremely uncomfortable and kept saying, "No! No!"

As soon as the shears had cut completely around my heart, I had peace. Looking down, my chest had no markings indicating a surgery. Confused, I asked God what he had just done. He replied that he had removed my hard heart and replaced it with a soft heart. Somewhat confused, I said, "So, you can just do that?" Smiling, God replied, "I just did." I smiled and asked him why my heart had grown hard. He replied, "Cares of the world." I asked what I could do to keep this new heart soft. He said, "Be still,"

The Man Behind the Mask

which I understood to mean spending time with him.

God went on to tell me some things about how to help the man I had talked with that day, but I was also thankful for the soft heart.

I thanked God for the soft heart as I laid down to go to sleep. God gently replied, "Keep it that way." I smiled as I drifted off to sleep.

Chapter 11
No Turning Back

While I had experienced spiritual growth the last couple of years, my growth seemed to come a little here and a little there. But July 9, 2013, was to be one of those times I look back on as a significant landmark.

What got it started was a discussion during a Bible study the Sunday before. We were discussing how God is looking for fruit from our lives. There are numerous passages in the Bible that talk of trees (which we are compared to) being cut down and destroyed in a fire or cursed because they did not bear fruit.

While I was praying later that Sunday afternoon, I told God I knew I had fruit in my life, but I asked him why I only saw a little fruit. God immediately replied, "He who is faithful with a little is also faithful with much."

This reminded me of the passage in Luke 16:1-13. Later that day and the following Monday, I began meditating on this Scripture passage. As I was reading, Luke 16:11 suddenly jumped out at me. This verse stated that if someone was not faithful with worldly wealth, then no one would trust them with true riches.

The Man Behind the Mask

As soon as I read this, God reminded me of Luke 3 where John the Baptist was telling people to repent. When the people asked John how to repent, he responded with things like, "Whoever has two coats should give one coat away." Basically his response was that the people should be faithful with the natural riches they had. This baptism of repentance was to prepare them for the baptism of the spirit that was to come.

As I read these words, God prompted me to make a change in my finances. He asked me to begin giving my entire paycheck to him. My flesh was immediately uneasy about this prospect. While I did have some savings in the bank, the thought of giving my entire paycheck away was unsettling.

I continued praying about it, and on Tuesday I felt an assurance that this is what I was supposed to do. So I went ahead and wrote a check to a local ministry for the two weeks' worth of pay I would be getting on Friday. With the check written, I now had to wait a few days before I could give it.

That evening my mind was arguing about whether I should really give my entire paycheck away. After all, my mind told me, "You already give far more than most Christians do." I began reading Luke 16 again as these thoughts were still swimming around my mind. It was at this point I happened to read Luke 16:15, which says, "Ye are they which justify yourselves before men; but God knoweth your hearts." These words pierced my heart, and I immediately realized that I was justifying myself by comparing myself to others. At this realization, my spirit suddenly rose up, and I began saying "No turning back." It was at this point that it was settled. I would start giving my

No Turning Back

entire paycheck to God.

As soon as I made this decision, I felt something shift in me. It was like a wall or blockage that had been there just disappeared. I felt a new freedom. This decision was more than just about a paycheck; it was a symbolic way of telling God I was entirely his. No more holding back.

The next day at work, the change was noticeable. I no longer had the intense fear of man that had secretly gripped me for years. Things were different.

The first outward change was putting a plaque that said Jesus on my desk. You see, about a week before this, a retiring coworker had given me this plaque. But there was one problem. I was too embarrassed to put the plaque in my cube. Even after everything God had done in and through me over the years, I was still embarrassed to tell my coworkers that I was a Christian. And I was embarrassed about the fact that I was embarrassed. After everything God had done, I could not understand how I could still be ashamed to put up the plaque. Every day I looked with shame at the plaque that I had buried in the corner of my cube so no one would see it.

But now things were different. After this "shift" occurred in my life, I was no longer embarrassed. As I put the plaque in a more prominent location, I was not ashamed at all. Along with the fear disappearing, I was also filled with peace and joy. The work I did was no longer done to meet my needs. Everything I did at work was for God because I was not receiving anything for it. At the end of the week, I joyfully gave my entire paycheck to a Christian ministry. I did not know how long God would allow me to give my entire paycheck to him, but I was actually looking forward to it.

The Man Behind the Mask

The next week progressed; and I planned to give my next paycheck to the same ministry I had given my last one to. But God changed my plans when I heard of a need someone had. Immediately God told me a specific amount to give. Only this time, the amount was actually more than my entire paycheck. I was excited and hesitant at the same time. This larger amount would mean dipping into my savings, but there was no turning back. I was God's, and I valued my relationship with him more than my earthly treasure. What a joy it brought to be able to obey him in this way. It actually felt like I was really living for the first time in quite a while. I was discovering that life is meant to be an adventure, an adventure to be lived with God as we learn more about him and his great love for people.

By the following week, I was getting into the routine of giving my entire paycheck to God. At the beginning of each week, he would tell me what ministry to give my paycheck to. Whenever I thought about it during the week, I would pray for the ministry that I was giving to. As the days went by, I continued to be filled with a joy I had not previously had. And as the week came to a close, I joyfully wrote a check to that week's ministry.

Well, as always, now that I was in the routine, God shook things up. As the next week started, I expected God to tell me where my paycheck would be going. But the days went by and I heard nothing. I asked him specifically several times but did not get an answer.

It was during this week that I began thinking about all the giving I had been doing lately. As I thought about the sacrifice I had been making, some other thoughts began creeping in. Without even realizing it, I began thinking how God must really love me since I was giving so much. I

No Turning Back

did not recognize these thoughts for what they were, but I noticed I was having trouble coming into God's presence when I prayed.

So on Tuesday evening, I closed my eyes and quieted myself before God. I asked him to help me come into his presence. After about ten minutes, I saw a cloud. As I watched, two arms reached out of the cloud toward me. I felt God's presence as the arms came close to my face. Then, as I watched, the arms slowly turned so I could see the palms of the hands. There was a hole in each hand. Suddenly my heart was pierced with the realization that I was looking at my Savior's hands. Immediately the thoughts I had been having were exposed for the pride they really were, and I was reminded that God's love for me did not rise and fall on what I did. Certainly he enjoyed partnering with me, but I was not earning his love by the things I was doing.

After this lesson, the week continued to go by without God telling me who I should give this week's paycheck to. By the time Thursday came around, I became convinced this giving journey must be over and God was going to let me keep my paycheck for this week. My flesh was excited as I thought about the possibility of keeping my paycheck.

Then, on Thursday evening, I was made aware of a financial need that another ministry had. I immediately knew I was supposed to meet this need, but again it would be more than one week's paycheck. As soon as I decided to obey, my flesh got upset. I had been letting myself think about getting the money this week, and my flesh was not thrilled about the prospect of giving yet another paycheck away. But I went ahead and made the decision to keep obeying. Although there was a cost, it was far outweighed

The Man Behind the Mask

by the joy of partnering with God.

Giving my entire paycheck went on for two months. As I looked back, I realized my perspective had changed. I no longer saw my paycheck as "mine." I saw it as "ours." "Ours" in the sense of it being God's and mine. I no longer earned my paycheck and gave some of it to God. Instead, it was our paycheck, and God could use it as he desired. If there was some left for my needs, that was great. But if there was not any left over, that was fine, too. The joy came in simply partnering with him.

It was during this time of giving that something else notable happened. I was water baptized again.

You see, I was baptized at my church when I was probably about ten years old. Looking back, I can remember being dunked under the water, but I did not really know what I was doing. Although I am sure all the doctrine was explained to me, I know I did not really understand the significance.

In my late teen years, I thought about being baptized again. Every now and then my pastor would tell the congregation that he was going to be doing baptisms. I had a desire each time to be baptized, but I never felt ready. As my understanding grew over the years, I viewed water baptism as a commitment of my life to Jesus. While I really wanted to make this commitment, I knew I was not ready to do so. This always bothered me, but I was not going to get baptized for the outward show.

Things had changed now that I made the commitment to give God my entire paycheck. I knew I would still make mistakes, but I had come to the point where I had truly given my life to God.

It was at this point God told me I needed to be baptized again. At the time, I was driving home from work. Cruising along the road just a couple of miles from my house, God suddenly prompted me to get baptized. As I thought about it, I realized I really was ready. Water baptism would simply be the outward expression of what was going on inside me. I decided I would ask Pastor if he would baptize me. But God immediately knocked that idea. God impressed on me that I was to be baptized right away.

As soon as I arrived home from work, I went straight to the bathroom. Turning on the sink faucet, I stuck my head under the running water and said, "I baptize you in the name of the Father, the Son, and the Holy Spirit." While this baptism was a lot less dramatic than my baptism as a kid, it had so much more meaning. This time I understood going under the physical water was nothing more than a symbol of the real. The reality was the change of heart that was already going on inside of me.

As the weeks went by, I continued to hear from God and followed him day by day. Then one day in September, I found myself "praying to the ceiling." You know, when you pray and it seems like your prayers are simply bouncing off the ceiling. It felt like God was more than a million miles away.

To be honest, I am not sure if this happened suddenly or if God's presence had been fading gradually. But

The Man Behind the Mask

nonetheless, there I was feeling like an iron wall was between God and me. Not that either one of us had anything against each other, just that we were separated by a barrier.

I share this experience because I can remember hearing or reading about the lives of other people who followed Jesus. Many of the stories were about the great things God had done, but I always wondered what their lives looked like between the victories. Did they have struggles? Did they have times when they wondered if God could see them and hear them? I have already shared some of my earlier struggles, but even at this point in my life, there were still times when God seemed distant.

So there I sat, feeling like an empty shell. My prayer time that morning was nothing more than sitting there thinking about how awful this feeling of separation was.

The next day I woke up and had a prayer time again. Just like the day before, it felt like God was a million miles away. It was like I had lost all connection with him. This was not the first time I had experienced a time like this. In fact, as I mentioned in the beginning of this book, most of my prayer times felt this way when I first started seeking God. Many times I wondered if I had gone too far and perhaps God had given up on me. As I grew in my relationship with God, these dry times became fewer and farther between. But they still came.

Though he seemed a million miles away, I began reminding myself of what God had told me over the years. I remembered the time he told me he would never leave me or forsake me. Though it felt like he had forsaken me now, I knew better. I did not understand why God felt so far away, but I knew the truth. God was there just as close as

No Turning Back

he had ever been.

I began telling God how much I loved him and how thankful I was for him. To be honest, it felt weird. It really felt like I was just talking to myself because God seemed so distant. But going on what I knew to be true, I continued to praise him and sing songs to him.

After about an hour, I began to feel his presence a little. It was not much, but it was a relief. Over the next few days, I felt God's presence more and more as I continued to praise him.

To be honest, I do not know what brought on this experience. But I am thankful I have learned of God's faithfulness. No matter how things seem, I can always fall back on what God has told me. His words are true and reliable. The more I learn to truly trust God, the less the ups and downs of life affect me.

Chapter 12
Returning to Love

So here it was September 2013. It was now over six years since I had graduated college, but God was about to travel back in time with me.

It was Saturday, September 21, and I was mowing my parent's yard with their lawn tractor. The weather was perfect, seventy-five degrees with a slight breeze. The sun was shining, and there were a few puffy, white clouds in the sky. Just breathing the air was refreshing.

I was listening to the song "Chasing You" by Jenn Johnson on my MP3 player as I circled the yard in ever decreasing circles. I watched the grass fly from the mower as this song about chasing God and desiring to be near him resonated within me. I just wanted to hit a pause button and make this moment last forever. Setting my MP3 player to repeat, I listened to this same song over and over for about an hour and a half as I mowed the yard.

I was almost done mowing, when I glanced at a car

driving by our house. The car's window was open, and my eyes fell on the beautiful woman behind the wheel. At that moment, I flashed back to an experience that happened several years earlier.

At the time, I had been driving along a road in my home town when I passed by a lady jogging on the sidewalk. She had a beautiful body, and most of it was visible since she was wearing skimpy shorts and a sports bra.

Now remember, this was before God had done the deep cleansing in me. I was free from my addictions, but it was still a struggle at times to keep my mind from going where it should not. And without thinking, I took a second look at her in my rearview mirror as I passed by. I had to immediately reign in my thoughts as they started down a well-worn path I no longer wanted to travel. This constant struggle to keep my thoughts under control was frustrating, and I began complaining to God.

I asked God why he would make man to be so attracted to and enthralled with women. I mean, seriously, with all the evil that comes from man's attraction to women, surely there had to be some good reason for it. Right?

Immediately God reminded me that people are made in his image. Oh sure, we have twisted it up practically beyond recognition. But there still remains the dim reflection of our Creator. I was shocked as I realized God is obsessed with his creation. Just like a man can hardly pass a woman without looking at her, so God is attracted to us. He can hardly pass by us without looking our way.

Now I do not want to bring God down too low. He is holy and does not struggle with lust. His gaze is pure, and

Returning to Love

his love is perfect and completely selfless. But he desperately loves us. I mean, really, he died for us! If that does not show his passion for us, then I don't know what does.

So now, every time I see a woman, I am reminded of God's great desire to be with his creation. I continue to be amazed at the depth of God's love for us.

It was a few days after this flashback that God once again reminded me of his love and his desire to be near us.

I was having a short prayer time as I was getting ready for bed. God told me to read the first chapter of Song of Solomon. To be honest, I was not thrilled. I had read Song of Solomon before, and I was not in the mood for reading this crazy book of the Bible. But I decided to go ahead and obey.

Opening my Bible, I thumbed through the pages to Song of Solomon. My eyes fell on the second verse of the first chapter, and once again, I had a flashback to years earlier.

You see, the second verse talks about being kissed by the kisses of his mouth and his love being better than wine. Years ago I had heard a teaching on Song of Solomon. The preacher said we should take a verse out of Song of Solomon and ask God to reveal it to us. So I had decided to try it.

At the time, I was praying at IHOP. As I was sitting there, God reminded me about the Song of Solomon teaching. Deciding to try it, I opened up to the first chapter. My eyes fell on "Let him kiss me with the kisses of his

The Man Behind the Mask

mouth: for thy love is better than wine."

Immediately I felt very awkward. Asking God to kiss me seemed completely absurd. But I went ahead and asked God to let me experience being kissed by him. I felt nothing as I sat there for a few minutes and thought about how this certainly was not "better than wine." Deciding to give it up, I went on with my regular prayer time and promptly forgot about my request. I sat there for about an hour without experiencing God's presence. I was thinking about leaving earlier than I had originally planned, when it suddenly hit.

Out of nowhere, I began to feel God's presence really strongly. It quickly got to the point where I was rocking, my legs were shaking, and I was filled with a joy like I had never experienced before. The feeling was actually more like euphoria, but even euphoria does not come close to describing the pleasure I felt.

I was really glad the music was playing loudly at that moment because I started laughing quietly. It was so crazy. I was normally so reserved, and yet the joy was spilling out of me. I was trying to contain it, but I could not. It just spilled out.

This experience lasted for about an hour and a half. The entire time I was filled with this unspeakable pleasure and joy.

Finally, it subsided, and I sat in awe of what had just happened. But I had completely forgotten about what I had asked God when I started praying. Getting up to leave, I headed out the doors.

Just as I opened the door to leave, I sensed God smiling, and he said, "Now you understand," At that moment, it hit me! I had just experienced the very thing

Returning to Love

that I asked God about! I never would have dreamed how wonderful it could be to be "kissed by God."

In closing, I want to make it clear that "love" is far more than a giddy feeling. To truly love someone is to lay down one's life for them. God laid down his life for us, and we are to lay down our lives for him. However, God also enjoys spending time with us, and we should find pleasure in spending time with him. God desires that we would not just be his servants, but that we would also be his friends.

After these last couple of flashbacks, I found myself with both a renewed understanding of God's desire to be with me and a renewed passion to stay near to him.

This renewed love for God began to change my attitude when God asked me to do things. I was no longer asking God if I had to do something when he asked. Instead, I was thankful for any opportunity to simply partner with him.

The first opportunity came about a week after these flashbacks. It all started early on a Saturday morning. Waking up, I waited for my half closed eyes to focus on my clock. Realizing it was only five o'clock, I rolled over and tried to go back to sleep. But after lying there for about fifteen minutes, I realized sleep was evading me.

From past experience, I knew if I was awakened like this, there was a good chance God wanted something. So I sat up slowly and asked God what was going on. He did not reply. I turned on some worship music hoping to feel his presence. Again, there was nothing.

The Man Behind the Mask

Finally, I told God I could not feel his presence, and I asked him where he was. Immediately, he replied, "I'm at the clinic. Come join me."

I knew he was referring to the abortion clinic that I went to pray at periodically. "Really?" I thought. Didn't God understand it was Saturday morning and I needed to catch up on my sleep?

But I really wanted to be with God, so I got up and got ready to go. Looking quickly at the weather forecast, I noticed a high chance of rain for later in the morning. I hoped God would be ready to leave before it started raining, but I grabbed my umbrella just in case.

I arrived at the clinic about twenty minutes before it opened, and walked up to the sidewalk. Kneeling down in the early dawn, I started to pray quietly.

I had only been praying for a few minutes when some sidewalk counselors I knew showed up. Getting out of their car, they got things set up for another day of compassionate outreach to the women coming to the clinic.

I was still curious why God wanted me to come. There were usually several other people that came to pray on Saturday mornings, so I did not see what the big need was. But I was thankful to simply be partnering with God.

Soon the sun was up and the clinic was open for business. As always, my heart was broken for the lives that would be lost that day but hopeful that some might be spared by our presence.

After about an hour, no one else had showed up to pray. Looking up, I realized why. I saw storm clouds rolling in, and I could hear thunder in the distance.

A few minutes later, rain drops started coming down. I picked up my umbrella just as the sky let loose. But, with the wind and heavy rain, it did not take long for my shoes and pants to get soaked. Standing there, I watched the rain drops hit the mud in front of me.

"What am I doing here?" I thought. But once again I felt God's presence, and I remembered why. I was here simply to be with God and partner with him. If I wanted to hang out with God, then I guessed I better learn to enjoy doing what he did.

About an hour later, the rain stopped, and I sensed it was time to go home. On my way home, I thought about how close I had felt to God, just standing out there in the rain. I wondered how many times in the past God had to do things without me because I had been too busy or had not felt like doing it.

Arriving home, I thanked God for another opportunity to partner with him.

I went to bed that Saturday evening after praying at the clinic. Drifting off to sleep, I had no way of knowing God was not going to let me sleep in on Sunday morning either.

I had been sleeping soundly when I was awakened by the phone ringing. Once again, I looked over at the clock. It was six o'clock on Sunday morning. Thinking the call could be important, I rolled out of bed and walked down the hall just as someone finished leaving a message.

I pressed the play button on the answering machine and listened to my pastor's voice asking for anyone who got his message to please call him back right away.

My parents were out of town for the weekend, so I

The Man Behind the Mask

immediately returned my pastor's phone call. My pastor said he was not feeling well and was going to the emergency room. He needed someone to lead the church service and was wondering if my dad could do it. I replied that my dad was out of town so that was not an option. Pastor then asked me if I would be willing to lead the service.

As soon as he asked, I felt God's peace come over me, and I told Pastor that I would take care of it. Pastor also said I could call another member of our church to see if he wanted to preach.

After hanging up, I tried calling the person that Pastor had suggested could preach but did not get an answer. Then I tried calling his wife but still did not get an answer.

At this point, I realized what I had just gotten myself into. Here it was a few hours before church was to start, and I was supposed to lead it. And I had nothing to speak about.

I realized I had two options. Either I could scurry around and try to throw together a sermon and get some songs to lead the worship team with. Or I could just sit down and ask God what he wanted to do.

For a few seconds, I teetered between the two options. If I started right away, I could probably put together something to speak about. But, if I took time to pray about it, I certainly would not have time to come up with something on my own.

I sat down and decided to pray about it. I asked God what he wanted to do. Not hearing anything, I was again tempted to figure out something on my own. But I decided to wait on God.

After a few minutes, I felt God's presence. I asked

Returning to Love

him what he wanted to do. He told me he wanted me to share about his love.

Then God told me a song to sing. Only it was not a song I knew how to play on the piano. I told God that I could not play it, but God did not respond. Since he had told me to sing it, I decided to sing it without instruments. I had never sung without accompaniment in public before, but God gave me peace about it.

God then prompted me to call another church member who could play the guitar. I called him, and he said he would be willing to play and sing a few songs.

Finally, God told me to have a time for the congregation to share scriptures or testimonies. God also impressed on me Psalm 139. I was not sure, but I thought maybe I was supposed to have someone read it.

After getting these instructions, I told God I did not think this would take up much of the time, and I asked him what I should do if no one in the congregation wanted to share. To which God replied, "I've got your back." I smiled as God told me this. Here I was heading into the unknown, but I was confident in God.

So I headed off to church excited to see what God would do. In the past, I would have been scared and wishing I did not have to do it. But it was totally different doing it with God. I was calm and full of joy.

Once everyone had arrived, I told them Pastor was sick and then started the service. I immediately felt God's presence, and God proceeded to lead me step by step through the entire service.

My short teaching and song went well, and then my friend led some songs on his guitar. Then I asked if anyone had a scripture or testimony to share. There was silence. I

The Man Behind the Mask

waited a minute while thinking about how God had told me he had my back. I was a little uncomfortable, but with what God had told me, I waited another minute.

Finally, my brother-in-law got up and said he had a scripture to share. He walked to the front of the church and opened his Bible to none other than Psalm 139, the very passage God had laid on my heart that morning. I quietly smiled at God as I realized he really did have my back.

After my brother-in-law finished, someone else shared. Then others shared for about an hour. Not only did it take the regular amount of time, but we actually went a little past the normal time.

By the end of the service, I was amazed. People had opened up and shared. And others were deeply ministered to. Again, I was filled with joy to simply partner with God. It did not matter that it was something I wouldn't have really enjoyed naturally. It was a wonderful experience simply because I was doing it with God.

It was just a couple weeks after this that I once again had the joy of partnering with God. Getting home from work on Friday, I changed my clothes and lay down on my bed for a few seconds before getting on with the evening.

Lying there, I casually asked God what he wanted to do that evening. No sooner had the words left my mouth than God responded, "Go to Pizza Hut."

"What!" I thought. I immediately thought about how awkward it would be to go sit by myself and wait for the pizza. I could see ordering a pizza to go but not sitting there feeling self-conscience while waiting for a pizza. But

Returning to Love

I realized I had asked God what he wanted to do and not what I wanted to do.

So, as crazy as it seemed, I decided to go with it. I picked up a pen and a piece of paper. I thought I could use them to pretend like I was doing something while I waited for the pizza. Then, pausing for a second, I asked God why he wanted to go to Pizza Hut. He replied that there was a waitress there who needed us. Wow, now I was really expecting things to get awkward. But life with God is an adventure, so off I went.

I arrived at the restaurant. After a minute, a young waitress came over and asked me how many. I replied, "Just one."

Sitting down at a booth, I ordered water and a medium Italian sausage pizza. Then I waited. As I sat there, I did not know what to do. Feeling awkward, I occasionally took a sip of water and asked God what I should be doing, to which he did not respond.

Finally, after about twenty minutes, the waitress brought the pizza out to me. I ate slowly as I continued to ask God what he wanted me to do.

Looking down at my pen and blank piece of paper, I realized what God wanted me to do. And with God's prompting, I wrote a note to the waitress about how God loved her even if it did not seem like it at times. I told her that Jesus was real and she would find him if she would seek after him. At the end of the note, I also told her I was not writing this to make a pass at her but that she was beautiful and I wished her the best. Saying a silent prayer, I placed the note on the table along with a forty-dollar tip and headed out.

This is one of those times where the results from

obeying God were not for me to see. Maybe someday I will know the results of this note, but at this point, I have the joy of simply partnering with God. Life is such an adventure with God at the wheel.

Well, life was becoming more and more of an adventure. I had been obeying God consistently ever since he had given me the soft heart. And the more I obeyed, the more I was filled with joy and the closer to God I felt.

Then, in November of 2013, I hit a bump in the road. This occurrence was to turn out to be a learning experience.

It all started one day as I was getting ready to go pray with a guy (I'll call him Andy for the sake of the story). I had already been meeting with Andy for a while, and I always asked God for wisdom each week before we met. Almost every week, God would give me some insight that helped me minister effectively to Andy. Over the months, the things God told me were always right on, and my faith grew. I was always excited to see what God would tell me each week and how it would apply perfectly with what was going on in Andy's life at that moment. So, once again, I asked God if there was anything he wanted to tell me before I went to pray with Andy. God replied that I should take a birthday card to Andy. This surprised me because I did not even know if it was Andy's birthday. But I went ahead and got a card ready, and headed over to Andy's.

As I knocked on Andy's door, doubt suddenly began to flood my mind. I started to get nervous about giving him the birthday card. Without realizing it, I began to entertain

Returning to Love

these thoughts of doubt. I thought, "What if I heard wrongly and it is not really his birthday?" I did not want him to think I was weird. And I certainly did not want to shake his faith in God if it was not really his birthday. The doubt settled into my mind as I wondered whether I had really heard from God or not.

About that time, Andy opened the door and invited me in. Sitting down, we talked about the week, and I temporarily forgot about the card.

After chatting for a little while, my mind went back to the birthday card. I figured if it was really his birthday, there would be some cards or some other clue lying around his house. So, letting my eyes wander, I scanned the room for any clues. Seeing nothing, I decided I must have heard wrong. Shrugging it off, I decided not to follow through with giving the card. Without realizing it, I had allowed what I saw in the natural to persuade me to disobey God.

The evening went on, and our general discussion ended. Andy and I had our usual time of prayer, and then I went home.

When I woke up the next morning, I was not feeling God's presence like I had been lately. I was not sure what was going on, but I went ahead and had my prayer time and continued on with the day. But the spiritual dryness stayed with me.

By Sunday, I was still feeling spiritually dry, and I spent the afternoon waiting on God in prayer. As I waited, God reminded me about Andy's birthday card. Suddenly, I was aware of my disobedience. As soon as God reminded me of this, I was both grieved and afraid. This was the first time I had directly disobeyed something God asked me to do since he had given me a soft heart. Here I had hardened

The Man Behind the Mask

my heart, and I did not know if I would get a second chance at a soft heart.

In brokenness, I lay down on the floor. Lying there for about an hour, I thought about my disobedience. God brought me face to face with how serious my sin was. What might have seemed a little thing in the past, now seemed huge. It was not that I simply felt guilty about doing wrong; I was torn that I had done this to God. I highly valued my relationship with God. To go my own way was not what I wanted to do.

As I lay there, God reminded me that I belonged to him, and my disobedience was unfaithfulness. This unfaithfulness equated to adultery. My heart sank as I comprehended the gravity of what I had done. I had allowed my own thoughts to take control instead of simply obeying what God asked me to do.

It was in the midst of this sorrow that God told me to read Matthew 10:33. Not knowing what this verse was about, I curiously opened my Bible. My heart sank as I read the verse that says that those who deny God before men, Jesus will deny them before his Father. In trying to figure things out about the card instead of simply obeying God, I had refused to acknowledge him, and in a way, I had disowned him.

In fear and brokenness, I asked God to forgive me, to which God responded by telling me to read Psalm 103. Unsure of what I might find in this passage, I hesitantly opened my Bible. This time relief flooded me as I read about God's mercy and forgiveness to those who reverence him. I was so grateful to God for his mercy. Although I was filled with relief, I still did not feel God's presence like I had been feeling before I disobeyed.

Returning to Love

The dryness continued for a couple more days, but God broke through on the following Tuesday. At the time, I was listening to some worship music. As I praised God, I suddenly felt God's presence again. My spirit leapt inside me. It was as if I had been holding my breath for the past week and now I was taking in a deep, refreshing breath. But as God's presence filled me, I also noticed a tinge of fear. With this renewal of God's presence, I was afraid of failing again.

I told God that I hoped I would never fail him again. To which God replied, "You will fail again." I was taken aback. This did not sound like faith, and I really did not want to hear this, but I recognized it was God's voice. As God's words swirled around in my head, he continued, "But I will be there to catch you."

Immediately, joy and relief flooded me. As much as I hated the thought of failing again, knowing God would be there was all I needed to know. How great is God's mercy toward those who reverence him.

The Story Continues

And so, God's story continues, both in my life and the lives of others. I look back in amazement as I think of that day years ago when I looked over the pasture behind my house, that day when God told me there was more than meets the eye. At the time, I did not even know it was God speaking. And for that matter, I did not even know if he existed. But now I can say with confidence that God exists, and I know him. I do not know him nearly as well as I would like to, and not nearly as well as I will. For this one thing I do, laying aside everything that hinders, I press on to know my maker.

My prayer is that what God has done in me will encourage you to seek a closer relationship with him. He longs to have a relationship with you.

During a time of prayer in 2012, I was suddenly overcome with a tremendous sadness. At first I was confused and tried to figure out why I was so sad, but I quickly realized I was feeling God's sorrow. I asked God why he was so sad. He responded that his people did not know him.

The Man Behind the Mask

I asked him what I could do to help. He said, "Tell them that I am real and that I am a rewarder of those who diligently seek me." If you are interested, there is a Bible verse that goes along with that. It is Hebrews 11:6.

I would also like to offer a word of caution. God is all about a relationship and not a set of steps. In other words, do not expect to do the exact things that I did and see the exact same results. It is obeying what God tells *you* to do that brings life. We all have our own story.

Some people will give millions of dollars, others will give thousands, and others will give pennies. We should not measure our gift by the quantity. Luke 21:1-4 relates the story of a widow who moved God's heart by giving a couple of small coins. God is not after the quantity; he is after our heart.

In the same way, one person may preach on a stage before thousands of people, while someone else may distribute food to some hungry people in their city. God does not measure us by how big of an audience we have but simply by whether or not we did what he asked us to do. In Acts 6:1-6, the story is told of some widows who were not receiving their daily food. While the disciples were called by God to share the Gospel with many people, others were needed to take care of the practical needs of these widows. We should not strive to be like someone else. Instead, we should seek God and find out the story he has written for our life.

One time as I was praying, I saw God's hand writing a book. I asked what the book was about. He replied that he

The Story Continues

was writing the story of my life. This made me really curious, and the first question that slipped out of my mouth was, "Is it exciting?" In response, God asked me how it had been so far. I replied that it was not what I had expected or how I would have planned it, but it had been both exciting and good.

Still curious, I asked if my story had a good ending. He said, "Yes." Then I got puzzled as I started thinking about those who die without knowing God. I asked him why some people's stories did not have good endings. God replied that he did not write those stories. He went on to say that those people had written their own stories.

This really got me thinking, so I asked him how I could make sure I lived his story for my life and not my own story. As I asked God about this, I did not hear a reply, and I could feel his presence fading. Insistently, I asked the question again. Just as God's presence had almost faded away, I heard him say, "Man shall not live by bread alone, but by every word that proceeds from the mouth of God."

To learn more about this, you can read the scripture passages surrounding Deuteronomy 8:3 and Luke 4:4. But the basic idea is we have the choice of living our own life (writing our own story) or following God (living the story God wrote for us). One leads to life, and the other leads to death. The choice is yours.

In closing, I do not claim to know everything. I simply know God desperately loves his creation and desires to have a relationship with us. I have so many

The Man Behind the Mask

weaknesses and shortcomings in my life, but God continues to faithfully refine me.

Do not ever become content to simply live with the chains that have you bound. Run to Jesus. He lived, died, and rose from the dead. He is not a fairy tale. He still delivers.

If I were to summarize my life to this point, I would do it like this: Amazing grace, how sweet the sound, that saved a wretch like me. I once was lost, but now am found. Was blind, but now I see. Praise be to God! Jesus, you are my life; lead on!

About The Author

D.T. grew up in the Kansas City area. He has a bachelor's degree in mechanical engineering and has been employed for about ten years as a design engineer in the avionics industry. He enjoys reading as well as playing the piano and guitar. He is also active in his church, which provides housing and ministry to people in need. Although he still hides behind his mask at times, his true desire is to know God and make him known to others. While everyone faces their own battles, he is aware there are far too many who face the same struggles he did. His prayer is that by exposing his past, others will find the healing and joy that come from a relationship with God.

Where to Purchase

Additional copies of this book may be purchased online at www.amazon.com. The author receives no payment from book sales. Book price is only to cover production costs.

Contact the Author

I would love to hear any thoughts or questions you may have. Please send emails to: d3comment@gmail.com

Made in the USA
Middletown, DE
03 July 2016